To Graham
'in Appreciation
of your
friendship
over the
years.
Chris

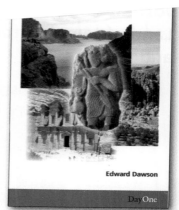

Edward Dawson

Series Editor: Brian H Edwards

TRAVEL
THROUGH

Jordan
Land of temples, fortresses and mosaics

92

ways, its high places and its 'god-blocks'. Petra opens a window on the thought-world of paganism in Old Testament times that the prophets of Yahweh preached against. Later, when Petra became a Christian city it seems that the temples remained.

Path to the Siq and the Siq

The visit to Petra begins with the descent from the official entrance to the 'Siq' or gorge. On the way a number of what are essentially ornate tombs, including the square-shaped 'djin blocks', come into view. Djin is the Arabic for 'spirit'. Two prominent unrelated monuments on top of each other are the Obelisk Tomb and the Bab el-Siq Triclinium, both quite near the entrance to the Siq. This Triclinium was one of the places for having funeral meals for the dead.

The 1.6 km Siq with its thirty-five water inlets, seventy-one sacred niches and other monuments could easily be blocked. Some of its Nabataean paving can still be seen. Little of the original arch that marked its entrance can be seen today.

Top right: Each 'betyl' (house of god, the same word as 'bethel') represented either a god or his 'house' or the god's dwelling place. Notice the platform for the god's dwelling.

Right: Towards the end of the Siq on the left is this partially destroyed carving of a camel and camel driver. At one end a relief life-size it would have been one of the largest carvings in the area.

Khazneh

The Siq opens out onto a view of the Khazneh (treasury), probably Petra's most famous carving, and best seen in the glow of the morning sun at around 10am or 11am. Of interest is the polytheistic nature of the façade. The Egyptian goddess Isis is centre stage below the urn at the top, although she could be a composite goddess for she appears to be carrying a cornucopia of the fruits of the earth (a symbol

of plenty) which is associated with the Greek goddess Tyche. At ground level are Castor and Pollux, who were the twin gods portrayed on the ship that carried Paul to Malta (Acts 28:11). The eagles hovering above the urn in the top are thought to represent the slain Nabataean god, Dushara. Immediately below the Khazneh are another layer of tomb façades. The Khazneh is likely to have been a tomb.

Who were the Nabateans?

Nabatih was Esmaun's eldest son (Genesis 25:13). The identification of the Nabateans with the descendants of Ishmael, while not universally accepted, is supported by some specialists and the would remind the Nabateans: Bararin history has further burdened years or so. A people called the 'Nabatu' are first mentioned in Assyrian texts of the 7th century BC.

The Nabataean kingdom, which bordered on Arabian (where flourished most spectacularly during the time of Christ. The mother of Herod the Great was Nabataean, as was the king-wife of these Antipas, whom he left to take Herodias (Matt. 6:17). The governor of Aretas IV was, be-

cause of Paul's greatest humiliation (2 Corinthians 11:32–33) Paul's 'Arabia' (Galatians 1:17) would have meant the Nabataean kingdom. For 300 years the Nabateans were a power in the area. As Arab nomads they were under a similar injunction to this given to the Rechabites in Jeremiah 35:6–7. According to a 1st century BC amount, the Nabateans were under an injunction the infringement of which was a capital offence—not

possibly for Aretas 1:11. The interest seems to be set up for the offering of libations. In front of it was probably an artificial lake (an in Iraq El Emir) thus making the overall spectacle even more impressive.

Outer Siq, theatre and High Place of Sacrifice

The route continues past the Khazneh through a broader gorge (the outer siq), coming

Right: Aretas IV from a coin. © APM, Jordan

to sow seed, plant fruit trees, drink wine or build any house. Later they did build settlements, but eventually returned to their nomadic roots. For a period, they controlled the spice and aromatic trade from Arabia and from further afield. They were among the world's most skilled water engineers. Fiercely independent, their kingdom was taken over by the Romans in AD 106. Christianity reached the Nabateans at an early period.

93

27

2 Northern Gilead—balm and crossroads

Like Bashan, Gilead was a synonym for plenty (Micah 7:14) and the visitor, seeing this attractive and relatively well-wooded region, can understand the two and a half tribes choosing it for their inheritance (Numbers 32:1–5)

Gilead was famous for its balsam and bountiful Jordan (Jeremiah 8:22). In the Bible 'Gilead' was a slightly flexible term, but basically included the area a little south of the Yarmuk river right down to the Arnon. Bounded by the river Jabbok. Of all the areas east of the river, Gilead is geologically more like its western counterpart across the Jordan. Within Gilead there were, as it were, an immovable enclave linked around their capital, which is present-day Amman. To the west, the Jordan river was Gilead's boundary, but the eastern border was a little more vague as the area opened out into the desert. At times the Ammonites and the Moabites wrested parts of Gilead and the area was also vulnerable to the marauding nomads of the east.

The word 'Gilead' has been preserved in the name of a village now Salt where there are some Roman and Byzantine remains. Just before the village, on the left, is Camp Gilead where Christian summer camps are held.

Amorites and Canaanites

Who were the people in the Transjordan before the two and a half tribes arrived? The

Ammonites, Moabites and Edomites were certainly around (see Numbers 20:14). But apart from them, the short common must be then the Canaanites lived in the Jordan Valley and the Amorites lived in the hills (Numbers 13:29). The people of Israel defeated the Amorites at Jahaz (Judges 11:20) which may be Tell Mazbyneh Thamad. Their capital was at Heshbon (see page 49). The Amorites probably originated

Above: The Jerash 'chariots display' gives insight into the Roman army at the time of Christ.

Facing page: This processional way led originally to the temple of Dionysius but it was left here when a cathedral was built in place of the temple

CONTENTS

© Day One Publications 2010 First printed 2010

A CIP record is held at The British Library   ISBN 978-1-84625-213-6

Published by Day One Publications Ryelands Road, Leominster, HR6 8NZ

☎ 01568 613 740 FAX 01568 611 473 email: sales@dayone.co.uk www.dayone.co.uk All rights reserved

sign: Kathryn Chedgzoy Printed by Polskabook, Poland

Welcome to Jordan—the other holy land

It is not often appreciated how much of the biblical narrative is set in the land that we know today as Jordan. Abraham's cities of the plain were almost certainly here (Genesis 14:2), and Jacob met with God at Peniel (Genesis 32:31). The setting of the book of Job was in, or near, Jordan and the final wilderness wanderings of the people of Israel ended with them travelling almost the length of the country from Aqaba up to Abel-Shittim, opposite Jericho.

Moses was buried on nearby Mt Nebo from where he had looked out over the promised land, and after the conquest, two and a half tribes settled in Gilead. Ruth was from Moab. When Absalom rebelled, David fled to Mahanaim, and later Solomon's ships sailed up the Gulf of Aqaba. Elijah began and ended his days in Jordan and John the Baptist ministered in the Jordan valley and, according to Josephus, was executed at Machaerus. Most of the Decapolis cities were in Jordan, and the Gadarene swine incident (Matthew 8) probably took place in the Gadara city state. Jesus' normal route between Galilee and Judaea would

have been east of the Jordan, avoiding Samaria. Finally, Paul's 'Arabia' (Galatians 1:17) was the Nabataean kingdom that, for a time, had its capital at Petra.

To learn about the Ammonites, Moabites and Edomites, we must go to Jordan. Rehoboam, included in the genealogy of Jesus, had Moabite and Ammonite blood flowing in his veins (1 Kings 14:21). Sites in Jordan are invaluable for a better understanding of the contemporary Roman world of Jesus and Paul. Today, Arabs and Jews are cousins and their shared cultural heritage opens up insights into the world of the Bible.

Facing page: Wadi Rum in the south of Jordan is one of the most beautiful parts of the desert that covers three quarters of the country and has been home to the sons of Ishmael for centuries

1 Far north—cows and oaks

After surveying the country as a whole, we consider the first of the biblical areas which Jordan spans: the southernmost portion of fertile Bashan

Jordan can be divided from west to east into three main sections: rift valley, highlands and desert. The rift valley is the lowest depression on earth. The highlands are a generally fertile plateau region which gradually peters out eastward into the barren desert. The highlands and the valley are bisected east-west by many wadis (valleys) and by four rivers: Yarmuk, Zerqa (Jabbok), Mujib (Arnon) and Hasa (Zered).

The country has three main vegetation zones: Mediterranean benefiting from hot summers and cool winters, Irano-Turanian which is the 'steppe' zone halfway between desert and good agricultural land, and Saharo-Arabian which is the true desert zone. Three quarters of Jordan is desert and it is among the ten poorest countries in the world for water. During the winter months (roughly November to April) around twenty-five weather fronts blow in from the west, bringing the possibility of rain. The rest of the year is virtually rainless. In spring and autumn the Khamsin winds can make life very dusty.

The northern highlands are the ancient lands of Gilead and Moab and are generally fertile

Top: Spring in the rich 'Mediterranean' type land of Gilead where the two and a half tribes chose to settle

Above: The granite mountains, south of the Hisma, the southern limit of Edom

Facing page: The remains of a fountain at Umm Queis. Note the imported blue marble column

Above: Looking out over the eastern desert from the city of Jawa which dates back to the Early Bronze age (3300–2400 BC)

and reasonably well-watered. In the south, parts of the Edomite highlands were cultivable but they are higher and more exposed than Gilead and Moab. The borderless eastern desert was an area that made the habitable areas vulnerable to attack by marauding tribes like the Midianites (Judges 6:1). The port of Aqaba is Jordan's one outlet to the sea. During Solomon's reign, ships brought goods up the gulf of Aqaba from the arab world and beyond.

The regions

In biblical terms, from north to south, the present country of Jordan includes a small section of Bashan (the Gadarene plateau), Gilead, Moab (between the Arnon and Zered rivers) and Edom. Ammonite territory was essentially an enclave within Gilead.

In the biblical period, Canaanite temples were found at such places as Pella and Dayr Alla in the Jordan Valley. Before the entry of the Israelites into Israel and Gilead, the highlands were under the control of the Amorites (see pages 21-22), two of whose kings were Sihon and Og (Deuteronomy 3:1–8).

Left: The gulf of Aqaba through which Solomon's ships sailed

When the Assyrians gained control over Samaria in 722 BC, the Israelites on both sides of the river fared worse than the other peoples of the Transjordan who, according to archaeological evidence, seemed to have retained much of their independence (2 Kings 17:24). After the Assyrians lost control (c.612 BC), the area was under Babylonian rule followed by a period under the Persians from 539 BC. They in turn were followed by the successors of Alexander the Great: the Ptolemies and the Seleucids. This was known as the Hellenistic period.

rom David's day, Israel and ilead were subject to threats om the east by the Ammonites 37), Moabites (p 65)and domites (p 78) as well as from e Arameans and Assyrians rther north.

bove: The area of the Rift Valley, n either side of the Jordan river d continuing down to Aqaba, as known human habitation since fore Abraham

elow: The finest Hellenistic building Jordan is the Qasr at Iraq Il Emir. ellenistic building reached a peak der Herod the Great

During the latter part of the Hellenistic period, the Jews revolted and established a kingdom on both sides of the river Jordan. Pompey regained the area for the Romans in 63 BC, under whose ultimate control it remained for several centuries. Trajan annexed the Nabataean kingdom, adjacent to that of Herod's, in AD 106.

Christianity came to Jordan at an early date. Jerusalem Christians fled to Pella in AD 70, and at the time of the Muslim conquest Jordan was covered

with churches. Church building continued well into the Muslim period. During the Middle Ages Jordan was relatively neglected, but re-settlement of the East Bank began in the nineteenth century under the Ottoman Turks who were masters of the area for over four hundred years. In 1922, after the break-up of the Ottoman Empire at the end of the First World War, the Transjordan came under a British Mandate. It subsequently gained full independence in 1949 and, under the late King Hussein, Jordan made great strides forward. This process continues under his son King Abdullah. In 1995, the country made peace with Israel with whom it shares its longest border.

Bashan and Umm Queis (Gadara)

Bashan, famous in the Bible for its cows and oaks (Isaiah 2:13; Amos 4:1), is mainly situated in present day Syria, but it includes the plateau region in the far north of Jordan, south of the river Yarmuk. In Roman times Gadara (Umm Queis) was known as the Athens of the East famous for its (admittedly second rank) writers and scholars. It was at the centre of a city-state with part of its territory in present day Israel, where the Gadarene swine incident probably took place (Matthew 8:28–34). The people of this town asked Jesus to leave their area, but the good news was proclaimed in the city itself (Luke 8:39). In Hellenistic times Gadara became a walled city and a member of the Decapolis (see Box: The puzzle of the Decapolis). It was seized by the Jews during the 2nd century BC but recaptured by Pompey in 63 BC. Subsequently Gadara was re-taken by the Jews and then reverted to Roman rule in AD 69 after its recapture under the

The puzzle of the Decapolis

Decapolis means 'ten cities' in Greek and they represent a puzzle. We don't know when this seemingly loose alliance started. The first clear written references to it are in the gospels (Matthew 4:25; Mark 5:20; 7:31), but the member cities were Greek, mostly established in the Hellenistic era. Roman-era specialist, Tom Parker, suggests that by the end of the 1st century AD they formed an administrative district attached to the Roman province of Syria under the supervision of a single imperial official, each city having considerable independence. Membership varied over the centuries, and was not limited to ten. We do not know exactly the nature of their relationship; were they bound by a treaty to defend each other? Nor do we know where they were all located.

What we do know is that most of the cities were in Gilead: Pella, Capitolias (Bayt Ras), Gadara (Umm Queis), Abila, Jerash and Amman. By the time of Christ, they had given their name to the area east of the sea of Galilee even though one city, Beishan, was on the west side of the river and the term included three cities (Qanawat, Damascus and Dion) in modern day Syria and a second city in present day Israel (Hippos/ Sussita).

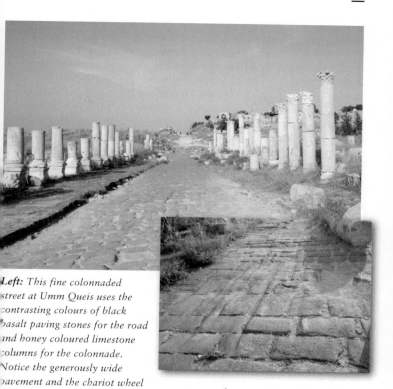

Left: This fine colonnaded street at Umm Queis uses the contrasting colours of black basalt paving stones for the road and honey coloured limestone columns for the colonnade. Notice the generously wide pavement and the chariot wheel ruts in the inset picture

Roman EmperorVespasian. Christianity became well established in Gadara at an early date and it was one of the few Jordanian cities to send a bishop to the Council of Nicaea in AD 325.

With views over the Sea of Galilee and the Golan Heights, a walk through the ancient city of Umm Queis is an unforgettable experience, especially at sunset. Appropriately, it is one of the best places in Jordan for seeing on-site ornate Roman-era tombs and grave complexes.

Flanked by the city's Hellenistic walls, the visitor can leave the car park and proceed west via the ticket office along a path that passes the unobtrusively restored basalt North Theatre, with its suggested 3,600 spectator capacity. Notice the more prestigious seats with their moulded backs at the top. Continuing along this path, the visitor will see fourteen Roman shop entrances on the right, and will then arrive at the main east-west road known as the Decumanus Maximus which is around 1.7 km (1 mi) in total.

Above the shops the visitor has just passed, is the basilica church with its octagonal interior, which is actually the first of two adjacent churches. The second three-aisled church is behind it. Further east along the road, the visitor will reach the

Temples

Jordan is an excellent place for seeing temples. Pella has a fine Old Testament era fortress temple. Shrines or small temples have been excavated at Ataruz, Mudaynah-Thamad and Tell il Umayri. At Petra there were three major Nabataean temples dating roughly to the time of Christ, and individual examples at Rabbah, Lehun, Rum, Dhat Ras, Khirbet adh-Dharih and Khirbet Tannur. Hellenistic and Roman era temples or sanctuaries have been found at Humayma, Petra, Amman, Jerash and Umm Queis.

There are similarities between pagan temples and the temples built by Solomon and Herod. There was a holy area, a sanctuary, with an inner holy of holies which in the case of pagan temples would contain an image of the god. The third element in a typical temple, the outer courtyard (or temenos) was most obvious in Roman times when it contributed greatly to the grandeur of the temple complex. It is important to remember that the temenos was an integral part of the whole temple complex; hence Jesus' anger at the buying and selling that took place in the temple courtyards (Matthew 21:12–13). In Jerash, the temple of Artemis (the Greek goddess so revered in Ephesus as Acts 19 indicates)

has something of the grandeur of Herod's temple, when taken together with its processional way and temenos—however, the visitor needs to use imagination to fill in the sections no longer there!

Another feature of temples was the presence of altars for animal sacrifices and incense offerings. The altar for sacrificing animals would generally be outside the main sanctuary, whilst incense altars could be in the sanctuaries themselves, sometimes within the holy of holies. A processional way might lead up to the temple, as at Jerash and Amman. According to Hebrews 8 and 9 the tabernacle and Solomon's temple have features which illustrate facets of Christ's sacrificial work for us on the cross.

Left: The sanctuary of the temple complex at Jerash

scant remains of two successive temples to the chief Greek god Zeus, below the main theatre (which itself is in a poor state of repair). The more obvious temple remains are on a raised platform and they date to the 2nd century BC; the remains nearer the theatre are from 2nd century AD. In their day, the successive

temples would have been impressive constructions, visible from afar.

Walking up over the rim of the theatre, the visitor comes to the museum. The objects on display are mostly Roman, some from the time of Jesus. In the first display room, immediately to the right of the entrance, is a

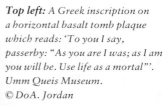

Top left: A Greek inscription on a horizontal basalt tomb plaque which reads: 'To you I say, passerby: "As you are I was; as I am you will be. Use life as a mortal"'. Umm Queis Museum. © DoA. Jordan

Middle left: A wheat grinder from the time of Christ typical of those used throughout the Roman world. © DoA. Jordan

Below: The headless goddess Tyche. Each city would have a protecting god or goddesss, and a lack of conformity to whatever would keep that god happy would often render Christians vulnerable to persecution. © DoA. Jordan

...et of medical instruments, such as those Luke might have used. Among the statues in the second display room, in the north-west of the museum courtyard, is one of the goddess known to the Greeks as Artemis; the Romans knew her as Diana. There are also several coffins and a few very heavy, but functioning, basalt doors.

Leaving the museum, the visitor should go down the hill along the path away from the theatre and will come to a locked Roman water tunnel to the right. It is worth walking down there and looking through the railings as it is possible to make out the marks on the chalk made by the Roman builders. This was one of two water tunnels serving the city. Gadara was part of a remarkable 170 km (106 mi) system of aqueducts and tunnels built by the Romans in the 2nd and 3rd centuries AD, which included the longest known tunnel system in the whole of the ancient world. In

Left: The large peristyle (courtyard with columns) gives some idea of the size of a major public area of the city of Umm Queis

the north of Jordan, you can peer down some of the excavation shafts used in the construction of the tunnel. Further down on the right, there is another tomb complex immediately next to the locked gate at the bottom, with stone coffins strewn over the ground. Pushing the heavy stone door you can enter and see more coffins and burial chambers.

Outside the site, on the opposite side of the road that leads to the car park, there are two more adjacent ornate tombs complete with inscriptions. Retracing back to the churches

above the shops, the visitor turning west will come to the Roman-Byzantine baths a hundred metres to the south of the main street. Continuing along the road, on the left there is a pagan shrine. Further still along the road, on the left, is an octagonal courtyard, which may well have been the meat market. Alongside the main street, by this courtyard, are more shops.

Behind the octagonal courtyard is a large rectangular public area flanked by columns with two smaller public spaces adjoining it to the west, one of

Above left: The locked entrances to a water tunnel at Umm Queis. With no rain for five months, cities depended on outside sources for water

Above right: One of the ornate tombs at Umm Queis

Right: An olive grove in north Jordan

which had a fountain and four costly imported marble columns in it. The dimensions of the large courtyard (approximately 70 by 55 metres/76 by 60 yards) help the visitor get a feel for the size of the city. Behind the main courtyard are the partially excavated remains of a bath complex. Notice the fine marble used in the flooring. The early city gate and a section of early city wall help frame this area. Opposite the city gate on the other side of the road is a domestic area under excavation

which includes the probable remains of another church.

As the visitor continues walking west, on the left is a church, originally 4th century AD, commemorating the Gadarene swine incident. Immediately below it is an intact, but locked, Roman mausoleum which later became a Christian burial place. Between the road and the mausoleum is the huge circular base of one end of a ceremonial arch, the Tiberias gate, which marked the beginning of the road that

Left: Part of the forum at Capitolias (Bayt Ras), the openings you see are for nine shops

Two other Decapolis cities

Capitolias (known today as Bayt Ras) was a large Decapolis city that seemingly has been continuously occupied since its foundation, or re-foundation, in AD 97/98. The Gentile nature of the area is well illustrated by the derivation of its name from that of the chief Roman god, Jupiter Capitolinus. The walled Roman city of 19 hectares (51 acres) is today largely covered in houses. There is also a fine theatre being currently excavated and a reservoir.

Abila

Unlike Bayt Ras, Abila was a Decapolis city at the time of Christ. Like Gadara it was 'liberated' from the Jews by Pompey in 63 BC. The population is estimated to have been around 8,000 people at the time of Christ. It is in a delightful location, among olive trees, and immediately above Wadi Quailibah which now encloses a pomegranate orchard. On the evidence of coins and other artefacts, it seems that a number of gods, of whom Hercules (son of chief god Zeus) was most prominent, were worshipped at Abila before the Christian era.

Of the remains that can be seen today, the large theatre has been largely stripped of its stones. There are the remains of a nymphaeum (literally a 'temple of the nymphs' but practically a place of pools where people could relax and enjoy

led down to that Galilean city, established a little after Christ. Further west, outside the enclosed area, are the scant remains of a hippodrome where chariot races were held, and behind it, another ceremonial arch.

Dar As-Saraya Museum

The excellent Dar As-Saraya museum is situated in an old Ottoman castle on the top of Tell Irbid in the centre of the city of Irbid. For the Bible student, there are a number of items providing a better picture of Canaanite culture, including pitchers reminiscent of the Gideon story (Judges 7:16), daily kitchen vessels and even some iron shackles (no doubt like Samson's although his were of bronze). The small statues gallery includes that of a Gadarene intellectual, called the 'philosopher', reminding us of the city's cultural importance. A section of city wall has been uncovered in one of the open courtyards, which also contains stone doors, coffins and a stone block with concave shapes carved into it used for measuring the volume of containers of liquids.

themselves), a bath complex and five excavated churches including an unusual one with five apses. The main remains on the citadel (the highest point) are of a Byzantine church, but it is thought there was a Greek temple there in earlier times. It is very possible that people from this town were among those from the Decapolis who followed Jesus (Matthew 4:25).

Umm el-Jimal

The city of Umm el-Jimal is typical of biblical Bashan; it is perhaps the most accessible place in Jordan to experience the basalt scenery that tends to characterise this region. Umm el-Jimal itself became a homely Byzantine market town after it lost its role as a Roman frontier fortress that kept the barbarians at bay. Although Umm el-Jimal is a town in ruins, buildings rise above their foundations, sometimes as high as five or six storeys. It contains over 150 buildings whose preservation extends to window frames, stairs, doors and roofs.

According to Bert De Vries (the leader of the archaeological teams that excavated the city): 'Umm el-Jimal is ordinary, a symbol of the real life of Rome's subjects. Umm el-Jimal gives us a glimpse of local people, Arabs, Nabataeans, Syrians, living ordinary lives.' Probably most of the inhabitants were Arabs and this makes Umm el-Jimal a significant early Arab Christian town, with its fifteen churches, dating from the 4th or 5th centuries AD onwards. The visitor can wander along its curving streets and realise how different Umm el-Jimal was from Jerash, much of which dates to the same period. One of the best preserved churches is the West Church. The visitor can also visit the main reservoir, 'the barracks' (a later Roman fortress building), the praetorium (the governor's building), private houses (in some of which the family would have lived on the first floor leaving the ground floor for animals) and other churches.

Right: The praetorium (governor's residence) at Umm el-Jimal

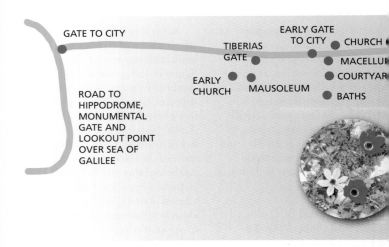

GATE TO CITY

EARLY GATE TO CITY

CHURCH

TIBERIAS GATE

MACELLU

COURTYAR

EARLY CHURCH

MAUSOLEUM

BATHS

ROAD TO HIPPODROME, MONUMENTAL GATE AND LOOKOUT POINT OVER SEA OF GALILEE

SITE PLAN OF UMM QUEIS

TRAVEL INFORMATION

For **Umm Queis** take the Jerash road from Amman and instead of turning off for Jerash go on up to Irbid and follow the brown and blue signs in Irbid for Umm Queis. The route through Irbid is not that easy and if in doubt, ask. Public transport from Amman is by an Irbid bus from Tababor station. At Irbid's Amman bus station get a shared fixed price white taxi or bus to Irbid's

northern bus station. There, take a bus to Umm Queis or to Hamma (in this case make sure you get off before the bus winds its way past the Umm Queis acropolis and descends into the valley). Going by public transport is straightforward but allow a full day. There are good restroom and refreshment facilities at Umm Queis, including a quality restaurant on the site itself with fantastic views over the Golan and Galilee.

For a good **viewpoint over the Sea of Galilee,** go out of the car park and turn right after the first checkpoint where you will come to a second checkpoint. Surrender your passport there in exchange for a paper in Arabic which you present at the third checkpoint further along this road. On the way to the third checkpoint you will pass the hippodrome and the ceremonial arch. The viewpoint is a little further on at what looks like a helicopter pad. On a good day it is worth the trouble as the views can be stunning.

The **Dar As-Saraya Museum** is not currently signposted. Head for the

Left: Five apse church at Abila

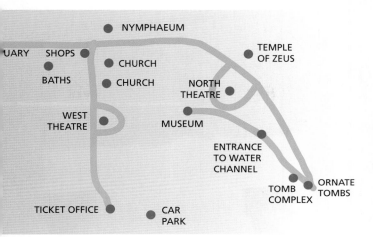

NYMPHAEUM

TEMPLE
OF ZEUS

UARY   SHOPS

CHURCH

BATHS   CHURCH

NORTH
THEATRE

WEST
THEATRE

MUSEUM

ENTRANCE
TO WATER
CHANNEL

ORNATE
TOMBS

TOMB
COMPLEX

TICKET OFFICE

CAR
PARK

ntre of Irbid and keep
look out for the ancient
tadel which stands
ove the surrounding
ban area. It is opposite
e Irbid municipality
uilding. Once at the
tadel, enter the museum
nd ask them to let
ou park in allocated
arking places for the
useum (signposted in
rabic only!)
www.dam.gov.jo
☎ +962 27245613
Capitolias (Bayt Ras).
ayt Ras is signposted
nd is 2 km after the final
orthern roundabout in
bid (characterised by
monument consisting
f interlocking pink
lindrical structures)
s you take the road for
mm Queis. The forum
nd museum are on the
entral road that leads to

the end of the plateau.
For the theatre, just
before the museum, turn
right past a school and
you will see it on your left.
If you turn left just before
the final rise at the end
of the promontory that
marks the limit of the city,
among the houses, you
will come to the remains
of a large reservoir.

For **Abila** take the
right hand fork at the first
traffic lights north of the
final Irbid roundabout
mentioned above. Go
along this road for 6.7
km and turn left at the
junction marked by a
mosque. After 0.8 km
notice on your left the

two water tunnels cut out
of the limestone. After a
further 0.9 km turn right
and go around an olive
grove to reach the site;
you should now be able to
see the columns. Enough
of the site is unlocked
to make it worth a visit.
If the caretaker is there
he can let you in to the
locked church ruins.
www.abila.org is the
website of the Abila
Archaeological Project.

For **Umm el-Jimal**
take the main road east
out of Amman and follow
the signs for the Syrian
border. The turn off for
Umm el-Jimal is marked
from this road.

ight: Vegetation of rich Gilead
rra rosa soil

② Northern Gilead—balm and crossroads

Like Bashan, Gilead was a synonym for plenty (Micah 7:14) and the visitor, seeing this attractive and relatively well-watered region, can understand the two and a half tribes choosing it for their inheritance (Numbers 32:1–5)

Gilead was famous for its hitherto unidentifiable balm (Jeremiah 8:22). In the Bible 'Gilead' was a slightly flexible term, but basically included the area a little south of the Yarmuk river right down to the river Arnon, bisected by the river Jabbok. Of all the areas east of the river, Gilead is geologically most like its western counterpart across the Jordan. Within Gilead there was, as it were, an Ammonite enclave based around their capital, which is present day Amman. To the west, the Jordan river was Gilead's boundary, but the eastern border was a little more vague as the area opened out onto the desert. At times the Ammonites and the Moabites seized parts of Gilead and the area was also vulnerable to the marauding nomads of the east.

The word 'Gilead' has been preserved in the name of a village near Salt where there are some Roman and Byzantine remains. Just before the village, on the left, is Camp Gilead where Christian summer camps are held.

Amorites and Canaanites

Who were the people in the Transjordan before the two and a half tribes arrived? The Ammonites, Moabites and Edomites were certainly around (see Numbers 20:14). But apart from them, the short answer must be that the Canaanites lived in the Jordan Valley and the Amorites lived in the hills (Numbers 13:29). The people of Israel defeated the Amorites at Jahaz (Judges 11:20) which may be Tell Mudaynah-Thamad. Their capital was at Heshbon (see page 45). The Amorites probably originated

Above: *The Jerash 'chariots display' gives insight into the Roman army at the time of Christ*

Facing page: *This processional way led originally to the temple of Dionysius but it was left here when a cathedral was built in place of the temple*

from the area in Syria north of the Euphrates river and migrated west sometime during the Bronze Age. They were both sedentary and nomadic.

As for the Canaanites, Canaan was a grandson of Seth, Adam's son. But 'Canaanite' can also be used in the Bible as a generic term for the inhabitants of the land before, during and after the entry of Joshua and the people into the area. It was also a term for a specific group among these inhabitants. See Genesis 36:2 for the former usage and Exodus 3:8 for the latter. They are first mentioned in a text from Syria dating to the 18th century BC. While attaching an ethnic label to the ancient inhabitants of excavated sites is often not easy for archaeologists, the religious remains found at places like Pella and Tell Zira'a would be consistent with a Canaanite population at these sites.

Jerash

To get a feel for a Roman city in the East in Christ's time, there is no better place than Jerash by virtue of the wide range of buildings uncovered and restored While virtually nothing remains from the time of Christ himself, most of what we see today would have been familiar to him from other Roman cities in Galilee, Judaea and the Decapolis. Jerash was another city captured and re-founded in the Hellenistic period, apparently by Perdiccas, one of the generals of Alexander the Great. It fell to the Jews in the centuries before Christ and was then captured by Pompey for the Romans in 63 BC. During one of the subsequent Jewish revolts in the 1st century AD, the city refused to surrender its Jews to the Romans and allowed them to leave the city. During the siege of Jerusalem in AD 70 one of the leading rebels was from the city.

Jerash is situated on two sides of a stream with the mainly residential area being on the east side and the mainly civic part being on the west. All was originally surrounded by an impressive Roman wall.

As the visitor leaves the ticket office, the first structure that appears is the monumental arch, buil in honour of the visit

Above: The display in the hippodrome includes fights between prisoners. These are the kind of contests early Christians might have had to endure

of the Emperor Hadrian to Jerash in the winter of AD 116/117. Hadrian was a great traveller in the Roman East and this arch is

Right and bottom:
The oval plaza is
the finest example
of its kind in the
Roman world

Below: *A detail of*
the Roman columns
at the South Theatre

found in the Roman world, it was also built on subsiding foundations and thus was not used for very long .Today an excellent display on the Roman army is presented twice daily in the hippodrome, called **the Jerash chariots**. The actual 'chariot race' part of the show is rather tame, but the main section of the presentation gives a very good and accurate picture of the Roman army at the time of Christ. You can see armed 'Roman soldiers' in full dress displaying different attack and defence formations and also 'prisoners'

one of the most magnificent of such triumphal arches to be found outside Rome. The inscription, now on the ground, dedicates the arch to 'the safety of the Lord' (emperor). The word 'safety' is the same Greek word used in the New Testament for 'salvation' (*soterias),* and 'lord' (*Kurios*) is the same word used for the Lord Jesus.

To the left of the arch is the hippodrome, which would have held around 15,000 spectators. It was roughly 245m (268 yards) long and 50m (46 yards) wide. It dates to the mid 2nd century A.D. The smallest hippodrome

performing staged—and quite dangerous—fights.

From the hippodrome the visitor walks through the South Gate, the main entrance to the city, and should notice a fine section of city wall to the right. The South Gate was one of six gates and the walls had 101 towers. They are more than 3,450m (3,774 yards) in length and enclose an area of 84 hectares (210 acres). Immediately behind the gate is a newly excavated 2nd

Above: *The South Theatre at Jerash has superb acoustics but might have involved unwholesome productions even if it was not the venue for the persecution of Christians*

century AD market area. After the market is the beautiful oval plaza. Notice the concentric paving. There were around 160 columns encircling the plaza and the knobs on the columns are there to make the visual affect of the columns more striking. The plaza skilfully draws together the South Gate, the temple of Zeus, South Theatre and the main north-south street in a way that is pleasing to the eye.

To the left of the oval plaza is the South Theatre. Completed in the early 2nd century AD, it is reckoned to have held 4,700 spectators. Like all ancient theatres, the acoustics are superb and the visitor should notice not just the spot in the orchestra (the

Above: *This is not the first temple of Zeus on this site, the one we see today at Jerash dates to the 2nd century AD*

Right: The sanctuary at the temple of Artemis. There would have been a statue of Artemis in the large alcove in the sanctuary; the interior would have been covered in marble

Top: For Christians with a tender conscience buying meat from the Macellum could have involved compromise

Above: The Nymphaeum had water spouts falling into the small basins below the stage; notice the big basin in the front

flat circular area in front of the seats) where a person can be heard anywhere in the seats above, but also the acoustic properties of the hollow area on the bottom tier of the individually numbered seats. They can be tested by sitting at opposite ends and communicating in whispers from the bottom seats.

The 2nd century AD temple of Zeus looms above the plaza, with the main sanctuary behind several huge columns. The temple included the level area in front of the sanctuary which itself was also surrounded by columns of which few remain today. The temple is on a podium, or substantial platform, measuring 40 by 28m (131 by 92ft). There was originally a staircase leading up to the roof of this sanctuary. Situated at the top of a long flight of steps

Above: There are some indications of processions in the Old Testament, but here at Jerash is a visible processional way starting far below in the city and continuing up an imposing staircase

and surrounded by its temenos (colonnaded courtyard), it would have been an impressive spectacle. In the underground corridor below the area in front of the temple is an excellently labelled display centre which includes a model of what the whole temple complex would have looked like,

as well as painted segments from its interior walls and parts of an altar.

After the oval plaza, the main north-south street continues, and the first significant structure on the left is the Macellum (meat market), originally built in AD 125. This octagonal courtyard would have had food stalls around it. At the end opposite the entrance is a slab pitted with knife marks next to some carved lions. Notice the fountain in the middle. In the Macellum, how much of the meat would have first been presented to the gods? This is what Paul was referring

Left: Here the altar for the temple of Artemis was outside the sanctuary and the main courtyard

Right: The temple at Jerash built in honour of Artemis. This picture tries to show something of the extent of the colonnaded courtyard around the temple. The sense of space would have increased its grandeur

to in 1 Corinthians 8:7. Christians in Jerash, might also have been faced with the dilemma of whether to eat meat they knew had been offered to gods like Zeus and Artemis.

After the Macellum the visitor comes to the South Tetrakionia with four quadruple column towers marking a crossroads and consisting of a round plaza. To the east, outside the fenced area, are the best remains of a Roman bridge at Jerash. The next significant structure on the left is the Nymphaeum, a place of public fountains for relaxation, completed in AD 190. Small traces of paintwork can be seen in one or two of the alcoves. Before the Nymphaeum, is the first of two processional ways. At the top of this processional staircase is a niche shrine to Mary and the angels Michael and Gabriel, suggesting that 5th century Christians may have eliminated a pagan temple but, sadly, not the kind of idolatrous ideas that went with it. (see facing page picture on page 20)

After the Nymphaeum, the visitor comes to the Temple of Artemis complex. Although not all the parts of this vast temple complex still exist, when taken together they represent a religious building similar in magnificence to Herod's temple in Jerusalem. The whole temple area is reckoned to have covered an area of 3.4 hectares (8.4 acres). The Temple of Artemis was linked to the residential part of the city by a processional way that started at least 300m (328 yards) into the city and crossed the river by a bridge, continuing up to the main north-south street. Above the river this processional way is blocked by a church, but steps continue on the west side of the north-south street until they reach

Left: A little to the south east of the temple of Artemis is a reconstruction of a 6th century AD water powered stone cutter, the original of which is claimed to be the oldest machine in the world. The wheel in the picture was attached to a crank which operated the cutter

Left: Part of tribal identity involved one of the Greek gods being attached to your tribe and naming the place where the tribe sat. Here is the beginning of the Greek word fule for 'tribe' which would have been followed by the name of a god

Who were the Arabs?

They were the descendants of Joktan (Genesis 10: 26–30), Abraham's son through his wife Keturah (Genesis 25:2–4), and Ishmael (Genesis 25:13–16), Abraham's son by his slave girl Hagar. A number of the names in these lists have been associated with known Arab groups or Arab place names. Two of the most significant Arab groups mentioned in Scripture are the Kedarites (such as Isaiah 21:16–17) and the Midianites or Ishmaelites, terms which tend to be used synonymously (compare Genesis 37:36 and 39:1). Moses lived in Midian for forty years and married a Midianite girl. Later he was told to exterminate them (Numbers 31:2) after they had helped lead Israel astray. David's sister married an Ishmaelite (1 Chronicles 2:13–17).

Gradually in the Old Testament the terms 'Arabia' and 'Arabian' came to be used generically (2 Chronicles 9:14) and there were strong trading and other contacts in the time of Solomon. Recently some have attempted to place the Arabs, and more specifically Ishmael, more firmly in the sweep of salvation history. It is suggested that the prophecy of Genesis 16:12 has been misinterpreted and it should have a less aggressive meaning (see NIV margin for example).

The prophetic literature deals with the Arabs and the descendants of Ishmael in a different way to that of Israel's other neighbours. While Job may or may not have been Arab ethnically, his cultural background was North Arabian. Agur and Lemuel (see Proverbs) seem to have been descendants of Ishmael. One tradition, with strong support, counts the Magi as Arabs rather than Persians, and their gifts would certainly fit that identification. Arabians heard the gospel through Peter on the day of Pentecost (Acts 2:11). Many of today's Jordanians are descendants of this biblical people group and share in their cultural heritage.

the altar of sacrifice, approached by seven groups of seven steps.

Notice a small altar for votive offerings to Artemis on the side of the stairway by the main altar. After the altar of sacrifice, the steps continue until they reach the temple courtyard, surrounded by columns, some of which remain today. The main temple building is behind massive orange columns Earthquakes failed to topple these columns, whose slight movement can be seen by placing keys or a knife in one of the column cracks. The temple building would have

contained an image of Artemis, the huntress goddess and patron of children and childbirth, and this inner part of the complex would have been faced by gleaming marble. Artemis was the same goddess whose adherents in Ephesus caused such a stir when Paul was there (Acts 19). There have been no signs of any little silver objects made in her honour here, but it seems that, as at Ephesus, she became Jerash's most important goddess. The idea of a processional way used in worship is a familiar one in scripture (2 Samuel 6:1–15, Nehemiah 12:31–37 and Psalm 132).

Behind the Artemis complex are the flattened ruins of the synagogue church, so named because it was built over a synagogue, thus testifying to the presence of Jews in the city as late as the 4th and 5th centuries AD. A mosaic depicting Noah's ark was discovered here.

The visitor continues to the North Theatre whose main structure dates from the 3rd

Top: The pagan nature of Jerash society was apparent everywhere. Here is a small altar to agathe tuche *(good chance). Tuche was a protectress goddess for many cities*

Above: Part of the Birketayn complex which included a theatre (1,000 spectators), two pools, baths and a 2nd century temple tomb (outside the fenced off area)

Above: *The little village of Listib, the possible birthplace of Elijah*

century AD and which held around 1,600 spectators. The Greek words on some of the seats represent the names of twelve Greek gods and the Emperor Hadrian, and signified the seating pattern for the different tribes who each took the name of a Greek god when the theatre was used as a council chamber. You could not escape the pervasive reminders of the Greek gods. One expert on Jerash has suggested that there may have been rivalry between the supporters of Zeus and Artemis, with the supporters of Artemis triumphing and the fulcrum of the city being focussed on the 'Artemis' part of the city rather than the 'Zeus' side. In later centuries when the two bath complexes were built, even going to the baths would have involved being in a place containing images of the gods.

Beyond the North Theatre, lower down, is the 2nd century AD North Tetrapylon, a beautifully proportioned building marking the crossroads between the main north-south and east-west streets.

On the return walk, back to the entrance, it is possible for the visitor to see three churches together (south-west of the temple of Artemis) and the cathedral which is to the south of the temple of Artemis complex. The main church in the three-church complex contains Jerash's finest mosaic and is dedicated to Cosmas and Damian who were Arab 'saints' martyred in the persecutions. The name of this church is a reminder of the strong Arab presence in Jordan even before the coming of Islam.

The Jerash museum, which is to the west of the oval plaza and on the oldest part of Jerash going back to at least pre-Abraham days, contains the foundation stone of a previous temple of Zeus with the inscription: 'Diodorus son of Zebedee, builder'. The date is AD 28, close to the year Christ died. While one person with the name 'son of Zebedee' was building a pagan temple at Jerash, another was preaching the gospel on the west bank of the Jordan (Mark 3:14–17). There is a fine mosaic depicting the city of Alexandria, and other material that helps fill out our understanding of the Roman urban life at the time of Christ. Outside the museum are various sarcophagi and inscriptions.

For those with their own transport it is possible to go round the perimeter fence roughly following the line of the eastern Roman wall starting at the North Gate and ending up at the ticket office. Although it is not officially open to the public, it is possible to look from behind the fence at Birketayn, which is a kilometre or two north of the ancient city on the road to Suf.

Khirbet Mar Elyas and Listib

Nestling in an area of evergreen oaks and olive groves, Khirbet Mar Elyas is the delightful site of one of Jordan's largest Byzantine churches, on the summit of the hill, as well as an older church a little below the summit. The site is associated with the birthplace of Elijah which traditionally has been linked to the little village of Listib a few hundred metres to the west of the hill. This identification is based on Tishbe being a changed form of the present day name of Listib and the association by the early church of the nearby hill with Elijah. In the church itself, the rooms at the four corners of the main church included those for preparing the bread and the wine (see the vine motifs in the mosaics) and for baptism (see the font). There are more sections of mosaic which are usually kept covered in winter.

There are also burial chambers below the church. The site is in a commanding location in the heart of Gilead and on a clear day Mount Tabor, the possible site of the transfiguration, and the outskirts of Nazareth can be seen to the west. Unfortunately, at the present time artefacts from the time of Elijah have not been discovered at nearby

Left: The baptistery at the large church on Khirbet Mar Elyas, the hill that overlooks Listib

Listib and known occupation dates there only from the Roman period. However, if Elijah was not born there, his birthplace would presumably have been in a village like it as he is clearly stated as being from Gilead (see 1 Kings 17:1). The nearby Wadi Yabis is a good candidate for the brook Cherith which was definitely east of the Jordan and where Elijah was fed by the ravens (1 Kings 17:3).

Salt Museum

At the time of Christ, Salt was a significant Roman town. It was mentioned in Josephus and went under the name of Gadora. Three of the rooms in this very small but informative museum cover the biblical period and give a representative selection of artefacts used in everyday life, such as grinding stones, containers and lamps. In the room devoted to the Iron Age (after 1200 BC), the second one you come to on the ground floor, notice the clay sherds with Aramaic script. They are a reminder of the language both Jesus and Paul spoke and of the fact that for a thousand years or so the Aramaic language and script was the common language in the Middle East. Also notice th representations of humans and animals found at so many sites, something expressly forbidden in Scripture (Exodus 20:4). One of the plaques in the room shows what the temple at Dayr Alla might have looked like and also a typical house from the Old Testament period. Upstairs, a room shows a few finds from the Hellenistic (Greek), Roman and Byzantine (early Christian) periods including everyday items from the village of Gilead and a stunningly coloured piece of blue glassware from another village.

Ajloun castle

Begun in 1184, Ajloun castle is an Islamic era castle built for defence against the Crusaders. Almost before you reach the open area at the top, there is a mosaic on your right which points to a monastery or church having been on the site before the Islamic castle. The theme of the mosaic was the feeding of the five thousand (Mattthew 14:15–21). There are superb views over the hills of Gilead from the top of the castle. The castle, which is well-lit, also has a worthwhile museum which contains a few Byzantine remains from Khirbet Mar Elyas (see above) as well as older material.

Above: Through the Tetrapylon at Jerash looking towards the north gate

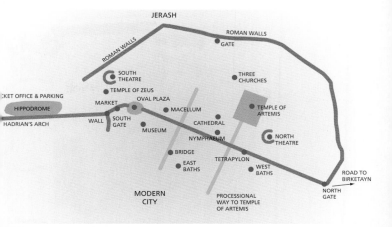

JERASH

ROMAN WALLS

ROMAN WALLS

GATE

SOUTH THEATRE

TEMPLE OF ZEUS

THREE CHURCHES

CKET OFFICE & PARKING

MARKET

OVAL PLAZA

MACELLUM

TEMPLE OF ARTEMIS

HIPPODROME

HADRIAN'S ARCH

WALL

SOUTH GATE

MUSEUM

CATHEDRAL

NYMPHAEUM

NORTH THEATRE

BRIDGE

EAST BATHS

TETRAPYLON

WEST BATHS

ROAD TO BIRKETAYN

MODERN CITY

PROCESSIONAL WAY TO TEMPLE OF ARTEMIS

NORTH GATE

SITE PLAN OF JERASH

TRAVEL INFORMATION

Jerash

For details of the Jerash Chariots display see www.jerashchariots.com ☎ +962 2 634 2471.

Jerash is an easy 50 minute drive from Amman. Go to Eighth Circle in Amman and follow the signs for Suweilih, from where you will see brown signs for Jerash or go to Suweilih directly. There is a restaurant just outside the site and limited refreshments available in the site itself.

By public transport go to the Tababor bus station in Amman where there are regular buses. Get out when most other people do) near the Roman Arch of Hadrian after the bus has turned left

to go to the bus station. Sometimes the Amman bus will be waiting at that corner; at other times you will need to walk to the bus station which is a little way out of town or flag down a bus going down that road back to the bus station to get back to Amman. You can also get a bus to Ajloun and Salt from Tababor.

If you are driving to Ajloun, follow the signs for Jerash and turn left for Ajloun just before you enter the city proper. For Salt, go to Suweileh and, instead of turning right to go to Jerash, go straight on.

Khirbet Mar Elyas is not on a public transport route. If you are going by car, go to Ajloun and from the

centre take the Irbid road out of the city and after 4.6 kilometres turn left towards Ishtafeina at a petrol station. Once in Ishtafeina, you will be directed to turn left for Khirbet Mar Elyas, but from then on the site becomes visible as the hill with the road that runs up it.

Above: *Second century market area by the Jerash South Gate*

③ Ammon—enclave of Lot's sons

One of Lot's sons has given his name to the area around Amman, a significant Iron Age city-state that was especially active in David's day. Through visits to its fortified cities and the main museum in the area we can learn more about a significant Old Testament people

In the Bible, the River Jabbok was described as the boundary of the Ammonites (Deuteronomy 3:16). This river, which started very near modern day Amman, formed the kingdom's boundary to the North. Madaba was the boundary to the south, the desert on the east and the river Jordan on the west.

Amman citadel

The Amman citadel consists of four terraces, one of which is now completely covered in modern housing. The upper two terraces, oriented north-south, contain the Umayyad (early Islamic) complex built on earlier Romano-Byzantine foundations and the buildings around the museum. Below the walls of the far north end of the upper terrace is one of the oldest sections of the citadel complex and it includes the covered cistern through which the attacking Seleucids were able to gain entry during the Hellenistic era. The remaining lower citadel is oriented east-west and includes Ammonite, Romano-Byzantine and Islamic remains.

A 9th century BC Ammonite inscription found elsewhere appears to be a dedication by an unknown Ammonite king of a temple to their god Milkom. This reminds us of Solomon's word 'I have indeed built you an exalted house, a place for you to dwell in for ever'(1 Kings 8:13). On an alternative reading of the Ammonite text the god Milkom orders the building of the temple, which in turn reminds us of 1 Chronicles 22:10 where God reveals to David that Solomon 'shall build a house for my name.' The inscription can be seen in the Amman museum.

Above: *This drawing shows Amman one hundred and fifty years ago. Notice the arch over the river Jabbok at the far left of the picture. In Roman times a section of river lay under a series of such arches*

Facing page: *A small restored section of the temple of Hercules on the Amman citadel*

Above: *A section of the Ammonite casemate walls on the lower citadel. Against such a wall Uriah the Hittite died fighting for the king who twice betrayed him (2 Samuel 11:14–25)*

Right: *On the lower citadel there are the excavated remains of an Ammonite palace. The courtyard of the palace is 10m by 15m. Part of the remains were two storeys high*

A bastion dating to the Iron Age was discovered near the palace; a bastion is a five-sided fortification allowing arrows to fire in many directions.

On the upper citadel, the 2nd century AD temple of Hercules has been partially restored to give an impression of the whole. Notice it is constructed on a platform and the whole would have been surrounded by a colonnaded area, the temenos, of which a few columns remain today. In the 19th century the propylaeon, the gate that marked the entrance to the sacred processional way leading up to the temple, was still in existence. Like the temple of Artemis complex at Jerash, the temple of Hercules represented more than just a central 'sanctuary' in which an image of the god was placed.

To the north of the temple is an early 4th century church, above a cave whose use goes back before the time of Abraham. Fifty metres away, a later and better preserved church complex is visible to the north-east of the temple. In the area outside the museum are some fine coffins, wheat grinders and two parts of what is presumed to have been an eight times life-size 13m (43ft) high marble statue of a female goddess, of which a finger and part of a shoulder are on display.

The visitor can then move on to the domed early Islamic reception hall, thought to have been built over an earlier Byzantine structure, partly because of its cruciform shape. Notice some of the fine decoration inside, which

Who were the Ammonites?

The Ammonites were descendants of Abraham's nephew Lot, through an incestuous union with his daughter (Genesis 19:38). They were separated from the rest of Gilead by the river Jabbok, and their capital was in Rabbath-Amman. By the time of the monarchy, they comprised one of Israel's neighbouring city-states. Their relationship to the people of Israel was that of a relative (Deuteronomy 2:19), a snare both to king and people (Nehemiah 13:23–27), executors of judgement (2 Kings 24:2), a threat (Nehemiah) and perpetrators of cruelty (Amos 1:13). At times Israel was victorious over the Ammonites (Judges 11:33, 2 Samuel 12:29–31) and they brought Israel tribute (2 Chronicles 27:5). They fared well under the Assyrians, to whom they paid tribute, but

Right: The small statue of an 8th century Ammonite king, Yerah Azar, at the Amman citadel museum. © DoA. Jordan. The latest Ammonite royal statue was found in April 2010

were subjugated by the Babylonians and subsequently became a province of the Persian Empire. They continued as a people until a century or two before Christ when, according to the Apocrypha (a collection of non-biblical books written between the Old and New Testaments), the Hasmoneans fought against them.

From Scripture and inscriptions, we know the names of 17 or 18 Ammonite kings. Their language was close to Hebrew and their god was Milkom or Molech (1 Kings 11:5). Alone among the peoples of Israel and Jordan, they were gifted sculptors of stone statues and their pottery differed from that of Moab and Judah. Like the Philistines they also used coffins with faces. Decades of excavation in the Amman area have meant we can visit Ammonite cities like Umayri and also enjoy seeing their craftsmanship in Jordanian museums, but lack of unambiguous religious texts means conclusions about their exact beliefs remain conjectural. Through his mother Maacah, Solomon's son Rehoboam was half-Ammonite and thus the Ammonites entered into the genealogy of Jesus (Matthew 1).

may well have been done by Christians at the behest of their Muslim rulers. Next to the hall is an early Islamic bath complex, but one that was very similar to the earlier Roman baths. A large Islamic-era cistern was almost certainly reused from a Romano-Byzantine one.

Continuing through the reception hall there is an open area that contains what was originally a section of a Roman street which leads on to the governor's residence. His actual throne room is relatively small reflecting the Eastern concept of glory (hidden away) rather than

Left: A section of the Dead Sea Scrolls on display at the Amman citadel museum.
© DoA. Jordan

the Western (huge magnificence). Compare this with the relatively small size of the Holy of Holies in the temple of Solomon. One estimate puts Solomon's Holy of Holies at 10 by 10m (32 by 32ft) out of a total size for the temple of around 30 by 100m (96 by 330ft).

Amman Citadel Museum

In the Citadel Museum, there are a number of pieces the visitor must not miss. The 9,000 year old Ain Ghazal statues are reckoned to be among the world's oldest representations of the human form. The 6,000 year old painting from Tuleilat Ghassul is interesting in that it represents some kind of religious ceremony. From Pella, there is a fine reconstructed ivory box with themes showing Egyptian influence. Also from Pella is a two-horned small incense altar with two representations of Astarte or Ashtaroth, a goddess that Solomon worshipped in his old age (1 Kings 11:4–5,33) and one that represented a perpetual snare to the people of Israel (1 Samuel 7:3 for example). From Safut is the so-called laughing god, a tiny figure whose identity is unknown.

Here also is the visually dull Balaam inscription whose importance cannot be underestimated in that it represents an extra-biblical reference to a significant Bible character who was not a king or ruler. The Balu stela (see page 67) sadly has a worn text that no-one has been able to read. An impressively large goddess figure from Khirbet Tannur makes an appearance. This must be the world's biggest collection of Ammonite statues, of which two 'two-faced' women and kings (one possibly a god) with Egyptian headdress are significant. There is an excellent collection of Nabataean pottery, including a charming group of three small musicians.

Because they were discovered in what was then Jordan, the museum contains some of the Dead Sea Scrolls including the famous copper scroll which contains instructions for finding buried treasure.

Beautiful Hellenistic pottery, a good collection of Roman glass, some Romano-Byzantine gold jewellery and some fine Byzantine pieces including a red glass 'fish' figure, help to make up a worthwhile visit. Last but not least, is the figure of Tuche, a possible city goddess with the city of Amman on her head. A new archaeological and historical museum in downtown Amman is expected to open in 2010/2011. However, it is likely that the Citadel Museum will stay much as it is.

Roman Amman

Amman was the southernmost of the Decapolis cities and was re-founded as Philadelphia in the Hellenistic period (not to be confused with the Philadelphia of Revelation 3). While it had most of the trappings of a Roman city of the time of Christ, the demanding topography presented a challenge to the city planners and much of Roman Amman dates to the 2nd and 3rd centuries AD and is either on the citadel or in the valley below.

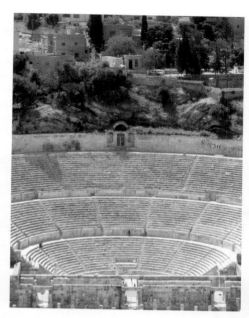

Above: The main theatre at Roman Amman could hold 6,000 spectators

Below: The small theatre possibly also a council chamber

There were two theatres and the odeum. This smaller theatre (1200 individuals), was probably used for poetry readings and council meetings and, like the main theatre, has been well restored. The two theatres adjoined a trapezoidal forum of 7620 sq. m (25,000 sq. ft) which made it among the biggest of Roman fora and was situated at the widest part of the

east-west valley in which central Amman is placed. Immediately in front of the main theatre is part of the Decumanus Maximus (the east-west street) which unusually had no pavement. Further to the west is the Nymphaeum which would have been a grand marble covered place of relaxation in its heyday. It was in the shape of a half octagon and contained pools, being built over a tributary that flowed into the river Jabbok. This river flowed through the downtown area and was covered by a vaulted arch parts of which remained to the 19th century. The vaulted covering was something of an engineering achievement in that it made more space available in the central city, helped communication and was also designed in such a way to minimise flooding. It is reckoned that the area of Roman Amman (including the citadel) could have been around 84,146 sq. m (276,000 sq. ft).

Above: A section of the Nymphaeum at Amman which would have been a magnificent structure in its day

Below: Restored Ammonite watchtower outside the Department of Antiquities office at Rujm ilMalfouf near Third Circle

Rujm ilMalfouf

There are a several Iron Age Ammonite watchtowers in the Amman area, a number of them surrounded and almost engulfed by modern houses. Rujm ilMalfouf is 'safe' being next to the Department of Antiquities office.

Iraq El-Emir

If its identification with Ramoth-Mizpeh is correct the tribe of Gad probably occupied this site (Joshua 13:26). It seems that the Ammonites occupied the site for a time.

The exact nature of the unfinished building, the Qasr, has been in doubt but it is likely to have been a fortified residence and it definitely dates back to the Hellenistic period. It thus shares some features with buildings built by Herod the Great and with those found at Petra. Josephus wrote about the Qasr and the estate surrounding it. Its owner was at odds with the Seleucid rulers of the period and ended up committing suicide. It is not clear whether the two 'Tobias' inscriptions on the caves on the right just as you make your final descent to the Qasr (or palace) refer to the same person Josephus writes about or to one of the Ammonite Tobiads.

Above: The main interest of the site at Iraq El-Emir is the Qasr, whose interior is shown here and whose exact nature nobody knows and which seems never to have been finished

Below: One of the two leopards guarding the temple; water would have come out of his mouth

An earlier traveller reported that a lake stood in front of the Qasr on which you could float ships; the present writer saw something similar when the area was temporarily flooded during a severe winter in the early nineties—although no ships! Notice on the Qasr itself animals, some defaced, which would have originally encircled the top storey. Also notice the two leopard fountains to the left and right of the main entrance. If the caretaker is there, it is possible to enter the

Right: Discovered in Tell Safut was the tiny laughing god, found in a cultic area. Now in the Amman citadel museum. © DoA. Jordan

building and walk up one of the staircases. Notice the huge blocks of stone used, some of the largest in the Middle East.

Tell Safut

Tell Safut is a very accessible Ammonite city. As the visitor descends into the Baq'ah valley on the way to Jerash it is on the right with the main road cutting through part of it. During the earlier period occupation was limited to the summit, but was expanded during the Ammonite period and the lower wall shows how much of the tell was occupied. Discovered here was the tiny laughing god, found in a cultic area on the site. Like Heshbon, Safut was another gatekeeper city guarding the King's Highway as it entered the rich agricultural land of the Baq'ah valley which can be appreciated from the sweeping views obtainable from the top of the tell.

Baq'ah valley sites

If the visitor turns off left from the Jerash road as you descend into the valley after Suweilih and follow the signs for Umm ad-Dananir, you will go through two probable Ammonite frontier posts, one to the left of the road and one to the right: Rujm il-Hawi and Rujm il-Henu East. They are the mirror image of each other and could have been used as farm buildings or villas as well as watchtowers or small fortresses. If you continue on the road for around half a kilometre and take the road left up a hill you will arrive at Umm ad-Dananir. Although there is little to see here, you can walk from here up the hill to Jebel el-Qusair, where there was a significant Early Bronze pre-Abrahamic settlement.

Tell Jawa

Tell Jawa is a 2 hectare (5 acre) fortified Ammonite town impressively towering above the Amman suburbs. Over 90 m (98 yds) of its casemate wall have been uncovered, as well as the foundations of some fine Ammonite houses. It mostly dates from the later Iron Age although it was occupied in the earlier Iron Age. Tell Jawa was not used during the Persian period although there was some Romano-Byzantine occupation. Because of its

Above: There are the remains of a substantial house in the south of Tell Jawa roughly halfway between the east and west ends of the tell. Notice the pillars and the stairway

Above: The fortification of Tell IlUmayri with the four-room house on the wall behind it

proximity to Amman, with its fine views, walls and house foundations, this little-visited site is well worth making the effort to see.

Tell IlUmayri

Tell IlUmayri is one of the most important and most accessible sites in Jordan for understanding the world of the Ammonites. 'Tell' means a ruin mound in Arabic. Umayri was a thriving town at the time of Abraham. It is reckoned it might have had a population of 1,600 and is one of the relatively few flourishing cities of the conquest period in the time of Joshua. It is possible that it was occupied for a time by the tribe of Reuben and it may have been captured by David's troops at the time of the war against the Ammonites

(2 Samuel 11:1). Situated near springs, notice the excellent defensive position on three sides and the section of superb wall uncovered on the 'easy' side of the tell. The fortification, which extends at least round that side of the tell, consists of a dry moat then a wall followed by a glacis and another wall. A glacis is a steep incline, in this case thirty-five degrees, which here was covered in charcoal ash and clay

Above: Because of objects found, it is thought that this area was some kind of cultic area; notice the thickness of the walls

making it very hard to negotiate. Then came a final casemate wall; a casemate wall is in effect two parallel walls with rooms in between them.

Here there is also a restored house on the wall, reminding us of a similar house belonging to Rahab the prostitute (Joshua 2:15). Notice the nature of this four-room house with a rectangular back room and then three rooms with a courtyard in front of them. One estimate reckoned that it needed 470 tons of material to build the four-room house: a mixture of stone, mud brick, mortar and plaster, branches, charcoal, ash, wooden posts. The house next to this has a 'sacred stone'—a large vertical boulder that was thought to represent a 'god' dwelling in the household. The people of Israel were warned against such practices (Deuteronomy 29:17). Another building that is thought to have been some kind of temple or worship place is in the area immediately to the north of the four-roomed house. Notice the high and very thick walls here. Several items connecting this building with worship of pagan gods were found.

The most important inscription to be found at Umayri was 'belonging to Mikom-'ur, servant of Ba'alyasha [Baalis]'. For the first time a name bearing the name of the Ammonite god had been found and also here was a clear reference to Baalis, king of the Ammonites, mentioned in Jeremiah 40:14. He was the

Top: The four-room house at Umayri. Notice the room at the back; the family would have lived on the first floor with the animals below

Above: A main area of interest for our period is the lower section of Tell Hisban where there is a two million litre reservoir. A strange feature of this reservoir is that it was in the highest point of the tell, meaning that all water had to be brought up there, presumably by donkey

instigator of the successful assassination of the Jewish administrator, Gedaliah.

In the Iron Age, the city was attacked and the resulting conflagration was so severe that some of the stones in the wall turned to lime. The city was occupied in the Persian period when it seems to have been an administrative centre. In the time after Christ it was occupied by the Jews as was evidenced by the discovery of some Jewish purification pools.

Tell Hisban

Tell Hisban is an imposing tell emerging out of the modern day village of Hisban. The first archaeologists to dig there concluded that Tell Hisban could not possibly be Heshbon of the Bible because of the lack of material evidence from the Late Bronze period. In other words, if this was the capital of Sihon, king of the Amorites (Deuteronomy 3:6), why was there no, or virtually no, evidence from before 1200 BC? Currently many consider that this probably *was* Heshbon because of the powerful association of the name. Also the lack of archaeological evidence could point to the nomadic nature of the Amorites. Tell Hisban stands in rich agricultural land and 'guards' a section of the King's Highway which passes nearby. A spring and stream would have been one of its water sources.

It is thought that the tribe of Reuben may have settled here, but in any case, there are Ammonite remains from the later Iron Age and Persian periods. It was occupied by the Seleucids and later by the Jewish rebels before being re-fortified under the auspices of Herod the Great. In Roman times there seems to have been an inn on the site. Christianity came here early and it was another of the few Jordanian cities to send a bishop to the Council of Nicaea in AD 325. There are the well restored foundations of a church on the tell and a larger one lower down in the village. Also on the north of the tell is a fine section of a Hellenistic-Roman wall with a gateway.

Tell Jalul

Tell Jalul is a large 7.3 hectare (18 acre) site with clear evidence of Ammonite occupation. It may also have been occupied by the Reubenites and it has been suggested as a strong candidate for the Levitical city of refuge, Bezer. Deuteronomy 4:43 describes Bezer as 'in the wilderness in the tableland' which would fit its situation. It is also a possible candidate for Heshbon!

Among the most interesting remains are sections of Iron Age paving at the east of the site. There is a large depression in the south of the tell from which a water channel ran; there are many cisterns around the site. On the north of the tell a three section pillared building with an intact wall was uncovered, the first in Jordan. Little of this can now be seen. In the centre of the tell are some excavated buildings from the Persian period.

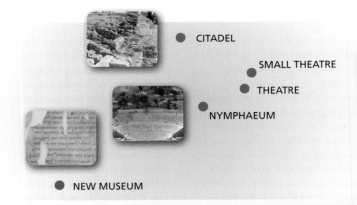

- CITADEL
- SMALL THEATRE
- THEATRE
- NYMPHAEUM
- NEW MUSEUM

DOWNTOWN AMMAN

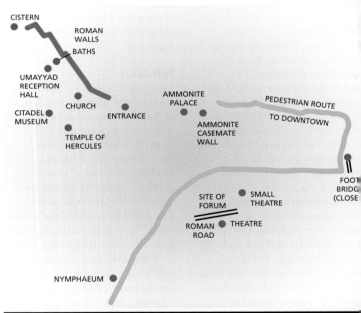

- CISTERN
- ROMAN WALLS
- BATHS
- UMAYYAD RECEPTION HALL
- CITADEL MUSEUM
- CHURCH
- ENTRANCE
- TEMPLE OF HERCULES
- AMMONITE PALACE
- AMMONITE CASEMATE WALL
- PEDESTRIAN ROUTE TO DOWNTOWN
- FOOT BRIDGE (CLOSE
- SITE OF FORUM
- SMALL THEATRE
- ROMAN ROAD
- THEATRE
- NYMPHAEUM

AMMAN CITADEL

TRAVEL INFORMATION

For an averagely fit visitor, the main sites of **central Amman** are all within walking distance of each other. Starting on the Citadel, it is possible then to walk down to the two theatres and the forum and, by continuing on the line of the Roman street westwards, to reach the Nymphaeum on the right after half a kilometre. The Nymphaeum is not officially open to the public but a good impression of the whole site can be obtained by looking through the fence on the main street and from the side road behind. Rujm ilMalfouf

Left: The paved road at the site of Tell Jalul

s at the Department f Antiquities. Coming om Fifth Circle go down Wadi Saqra and take the oad right just after the unnel. Take the second ght off this road and you ill see the Rujm. During ffice hours (from 8am to pm) the receptionist has he key.

Iraq il Emir. Go to ighth Circle and take he main road west. You ill first come to Wadi iir; continue through the illage along a road that ecomes much more rural or another 10km until ou reach the Qasr. The scriptions are on the liffs to your right about alf a kilometre before he Qasr.

Iraq il Emir is accessible y taking a Wadi Siir us from Mahatta or Muhajarin station and a econd Iraq il Emir bus om Wadi Siir.

Tell Safut. At Suweilih ake the Jerash road and fter roughly a kilometre ou will see the tell n your right. There is arking space there. is an easy walk from uweilih.

The Baqah valley ites are further on to the

left; take the turn for Um Dananir.

Tell Jawa. Go down the desert highway towards the airport and take the exit which ends in you going left at the sign marked 'Saudi border and Amman east', which is before the airport turn-off. Carry on this road east for 5.5km and you will see a green street sign saying 'Jawa street'. Go up this street and you will see the tell on the summit of the ridge. By public transport, take a bus from Mahatta bus station to Middle East Circle (duar issharq ilawsat) and a bus from there to Jawa.

Tell il Umayri is hard to reach by public transport although it is on the desert highway and you could take a bus from Tababor to Madaba and alight there. Getting back might be harder, but you could probably flag down a bus. By car, go down the airport highway for 11.5km after Seventh Circle and turn right at a cluster of signs, one of which is for

Aref il Faiz wood. You will see the tell on your right before the turn-off which is just after a petrol station.

Tell Hisban. Take the Desert Highway, turn off at the Dead Sea Road and take the turn-off for Madaba from the Dead Sea road, after a few kilometres. Hisban is a prominent village and hill on your right which you will come to a few kilometres before Madaba. The tell is signposted. **Do not** follow the signs for Madaba on the desert highway. There are buses to Hisban from Wihdat bus station.

Tell Jalul. Take the main road from Amman to Madaba and go straight into the city. Turn left at the police kiosk by the side of the road (just past a petrol station) and keep going for around 5km and you will see the large tell in front of you.

For the Umayri, Hisban and Jalul excavation sites see the website www. madabaplains.org

Right: The area in front of the theatre where the large forum was situated

④ Southern Gilead—land under changing ownership

Although Southern Gilead was part of the land of the two and a half tribes, at times control of parts of this territory swung between the Moabites and the Ammonites

The land north of the Arnon Gorge has furnished us with some named biblical sites whose identity is confirmed by three independent sources: Scripture, the Moabite Stone, and their modern-day names. Other sites, whose identities we are less certain of, have given us increased understanding of the Moabites (see Box: The Moabites page 65). At its greatest extent, the Moabite kingdom seems to have extended northwards to a line running east of the top end of the Dead Sea, but there were times when the Ammonites or the Israelites also controlled this area (Judges 11:13). Although southern Gilead was not part of their homeland, the Moabites were important players in this area for centuries.

Madaba

Although most of biblical era Madaba is covered by the modern town, two significant museums have preserved some of the Bronze and Iron Age, Roman and Byzantine material of the area. The northernmost museum (the archaeological park) includes a section of paved Roman road, remains of a Roman temple and the Hippolytus Hall from a Roman house (whose playful mosaic reflects classical themes). On the walls, are a number of mosaics from the area. In the less visited, but biblically more significant, southernmost museum are artefacts from Mudaynah, Khirbet Iskander, Ataruz and Madaba itself. As you leave the town going south, on the right is the huge mosaic of the Church of the Apostles. In the highest point of the town, in the citadel, excavations have

Above: Jerusalem at the centre of the Madaba mosaic map

Facing page: The Moabite Stone in the Louvre Museum. © Mark Connally

revealed Iron Age fortifications which could have been those made by Mesha who claims, in the Moabite stone, to have built Madaba after wresting it from Omri, the King of Israel.

Jebel Siyagha (Mount Nebo)

When people think of Mount Nebo, they are usually thinking of present day Jebel Siyagha, the traditional Mount Nebo. It lies at the extremity of a plateau rather than being a traditional mountain that you 'go up', although it would have been a long haul up from the Jordan Valley! The modern road from Mount Nebo down to the valley is well worth taking for the views over the Dead Sea and beyond. Pisgah, the Abarim mountains and Beth-Peor can be found on the edge of this plateau or on one of the hills in the immediate area although their precise locations are hard to pinpoint. What few would doubt is that it was in this area that Moses looked out over the promised land (Deuteronomy 34:1) and was buried by God (Deuteronomy 34:6). It was also here that Balaam ended up by blessing Israel (Numbers 23:14).

One of the major stopping points on the early church pilgrim routes, Jebel Siyagha

The Madaba Map

Discovered at the end of the 19th century during the building of a church in Madaba, the partially destroyed Madaba mosaic map would have used 2.3 million stone cubes in its original state. Moses was the particular 'saint' of Madaba and the map has been interpreted as representing his vision, not just of the promised land as seen from nearby Mount Nebo, but the salvation of mankind through the greater Moses. It is a unique and powerful visual aid that displays the linear salvation history of the Scriptures in one simultaneous sweep.

The sites depicted from both Testaments have been brought together in one place with Jerusalem, the place of the cross and resurrection, at the centre. The map shows over a hundred and fifty other places. Along with Eusebius' 4th century AD Onomasticon (a gazetteer of biblical sites), the 6th/7th century AD Madaba map has played a key role in helping us identify the location of biblical sites.

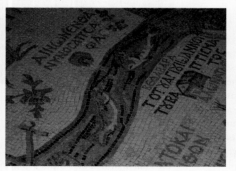

Left: In this part of the Madaba Map the fish are swimming away from the Dead Sea. Also in the picture is Bethabara, which some have identified with the site of Jesus' baptism

Left: Mount Nebo, which has been visited by pilgrims since the 4th century AD has been imaginatively developed by the Franciscans. Here is a bronze pillar uniting the snake and the cross in a modern design (Numbers 21:4–9)

ontains an attractive collection
f restored Byzantine buildings
specially the main church, with
s two baptismal fonts and
ne mosaics. The main church,
hose first structure went back
o the 4th century AD, was a
iapsoidal construction with
vo funerary chapels on either
de of the central apse. There
as a vestibule (enclosed area in
ont of a church) whose floor
as covered in a white mosaic.
ombs have been discovered
elow the funerary chapels. Off
ne main apse was a flight of stairs

*bove: The 5th century mosaic in
he church at Mount Nebo with the
aptismal font behind*

leading down to a baptistery, with a baptismal font and the mosaic that we see there today.

In the second part of the 6th century a new church was built consisting of three naves. A baptistery was added on the south side. Early in the 7th century the Mother of God chapel was built (on the right as you enter the chapel complex) which contains a representation of Jerusalem. Michele Piccirillo, the Franciscan monk who did so much to reveal the extent of Arab Christianity in the area, points out that 'In front of the altar… a rectangular panel with … two bulls standing before an altar surmounted by a ciborium [Eucharistic cup] can still be seen. The scene is explained by the Greek quotation of Psalm 51:19, "Then shall young bulls be offered on thy altar, O Lord". The mosaicist intended to depict the altar in the Temple at Jerusalem.' It is thought that he is indirectly making a connection with the sacrifices offered by Balaam in the Mount Nebo area. The fire in the mosaic points to these sacrifices. The temple pictured is Herod's temple in Jerusalem. The altar is not pictured but we are meant to imagine it. Byzantine mosaicists loved to recall biblical events and for this reason made a connection between Balaam and the temple of the Lord and the New Covenant. Surrounding the church was a monastic complex. The museum is worth a visit and contains a milestone describing the Emperor, Antoninus Pius (responsible for the Antonine wall in Scotland) as pontifex maximus 'High Priest'. There are other mosaics, helpful plaques and material from pre-Roman times.

Ataroth

Modern day Ataruz, is ancient Ataroth (Joshua 18:13). The Moabite Stone (see Box: The Moabite Stone page 55) describes how, at Ataruz, the Moabite King Mesha desecrated the Davidic altar hearth (belonging to the occupying tribe of Gad) and brought it to the place of his god Chemosh. Mesha was initially subject to Israel but later rebelled (2 Kings 3:4,5) and for a period seems to have had the upper hand in the area. Ataroth

was described as having been fortified by the king of Israel and was evidently some kind of city-state (land of Ataroth). A small temple consisting of three parallel rooms has been discovered on the citadel and one room contains a sacred stone and an altar in front of it. Near the citadel, below a modern agricultural building next to the road, is what appears to be the rest of the town with wall lines and ruins. There was also Byzantine occupation of the area.

Machaerus

Splendid in its bleak isolation, the Herodian fortress of Machaerus was, according to the Jewish historian Josephus, the place of John the Baptist's execution. A half an hour walk along the ridge of the hills past the fortress will take the visitor to a high point from where the whole of the north section of the Dead Sea is spread out before you as well as good views of the Judaean hills.

Below: The sacred stone at the Moabite temple at Ataruz

Right: Herodian fortress of
Machaerus

Machaerus was built by the mad Jewish leader Alexander Jannaeus in the 2nd century BC and captured by the Romans in AD 59. It was then re-fortified by Herod the Great who would come here from the Dead Sea port of Callirhoe; it was later used by Herod Antipas. In AD 68 it was re-taken by the Jews but fell to the Romans four years later in a capture that was graphically described by Josephus in his *History of the Jews* and is worth reading today. However, the visitor first has to walk up the hill itself.

You should notice on the right the foundation of a double-aqueduct which also served as a bridge from the Roman village of Machaerus to the castle itself. The impression on the summit is mainly of flattened buildings in spite of some restoration. Today these ruins include a partially restored colonnaded hall above a massive cistern and the remains of a bath complex that was better—it included a sauna—than the ones at Masada and Herodion. Some of the red tiles from the bath complex can still be seen. On the north-east side there is a plastered water channel that leads round to a second cistern in the north side of the mountain. As for the walls, they include the bases of three towers: one on the south, the south-west and the east. Outside the walls, on the northern side of the mountain there was the lower city of which little remains today. Behind the western end of the castle there is a massive pile of rocks. This was the siege ramp used by the Romans during the Jewish revolt of AD 68–72. If you follow a line beyond the ramp you can make out a square shape, one of the Roman camps built during the siege. Others are dotted around the hills.

Above: Roman siege ramp at Machaerus in the foreground. In the background is the Roman camp and the Dead Sea

Khirbet Iskander

Khirbet Iskander is situated to the west of the modern King's Highway where it crosses the Wadi Wala. Occupied for a thousand years or so before Abraham during the Early Bronze Age, it seems to have been abandoned in Abraham's day. Economic factors such as trade route collapse, agricultural or climatic problems or possibly the coming of the Amorites into the area could explain its demise. Including the settlement around it, the site covers roughly 4 hectares (10 acres). There are gateways in the south-east and the north west. On the hill to the north of the site, Umm Idrum, excavators think they have found a 'high place' (a place for worship).

Below: The Moabite capital of Dhiban very near the Arnon Gorge and also the King's Highway making it a strategic location

Dhiban

Dhiban was Mesha's capital city, and in the Moabite Stone he describes how he built a temple for Chemosh. Chemosh was the national god of the Moabites, but seems to have been only one of the gods the Moabites and other people worshipped. Moabite specialist Jerry Mattingly proposes an indentification of Chemosh with the Mesopotamian god Nergal, thus making Chemosh the god of infernal nature or hell. Another link has been made between Chemosh and Ares, the Greek god of war. Dhiban was also occupied by the Israelites for a period. Today, the southernmost of the two hills is covered by modern housing but the main tell contains remains from a number of periods. Attempts to find the temple Mesha claims to have built have so far been unsuccessful but there are some remains in the north-east of the tell of Mesha's fortifications. Some of the excavated sections also date to the Roman period and after.

Above: The gate at Khirbet Iskander dating to the era that ended just about the time of Abraham. Notice the bench on the right emphasising once again the importance of the gateway area in the life of the city

Above: The site of Dhiban includes a Nabataean temple at the entrance which is similar in design to the Qasr il Bint at Petra

Left: The Moabite Stone.

The Moabite Stone

The Moabite Stone, with its 34-line partially defaced royal inscription, was discovered in 1868. It is the longest Old Testament era 'document' so far discovered from the Southern Levant (Jordan, Syria and Israel). It contains a text from a period of the Old Testament kings that mentions Yahweh, Mesha, Omri, Israel, the tribe of Gad and a number of biblical towns. Its style and language were almost identical to that of the Bible, except that in this case the 'god' involved was Chemosh, the patron deity of the Moabites. In lines 17 and 18 Mesha claims he took 'the vessels of Yahweh and dragged them before Kemosh' from Nebo.

Later study of the inscription revealed a reference to the house of David in connection with Ataroth (Ataruz, see page 52). The description of Mesha's rebellion against Israel (also mentioned in 2 Kings 3) seems to have occurred at the time of the collapse of the anti-Assyrian alliance between Israel and Aram (the Syrian kingdom then centred on Damascus). This break-up would help explain how Mesha was able to rebel.

The nature of the inscription's discovery, which involved local Bedouin breaking up the stone to increase its value, only added to the romance associated with the inscription. It can now be found in the Louvre Museum, Paris, with facsimiles to be seen in the Amman, Madaba and Kerak museums.

Arnon

The most spectacular canyon in the area and the most important eastern river flowing into the Dead Sea, the Arnon Gorge is also a natural boundary which in biblical times separated Moab proper from Gilead. In the Moabite stone Mesha mentions that he 'made' the highway over the Arnon. The Arnon is mentioned twenty-five times in the Bible. Its border position is described in Numbers 22:36 and Deuteronomy 3:16. The Israelites camped there on their way through Jordan (Numbers 21:13) where it is described as the border between the Moabites and the Amorites. The routes across the Arnon were compressed into a 3 or 4 km span: too near the Dead Sea and you confronted a dangerous gorge; further to the east you had to cross three tributary rivers, and if you tried to cross east of these you were in the desert. This helps explain the cluster of cities and settlements like Dhiban, Lehun, Aroer and Balu' (on the other side of the gorge) all on roughly the same axis.

Below: The formidable barrier that was the Arnon is shown here where two tributaries can be seen flowing into the now dammed river

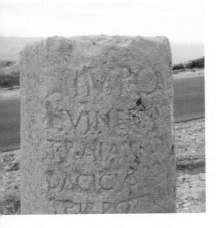

Above: Part of a milestone in the Arnon Gorge on the Roman road; it mentions Trajan in whose reign this successor to the King's Highway was built

Aroer

Spectacularly located on the Arnon gorge is the fortress of Ara'ir, which is biblical Aroer. Mesha, in the Moabite stone, describes how he built Aroer and made a road through the Arnon. Aroer is another 'gatekeeper' city overlooking this strategic crossing point of the gorge. Well protected by the steepness of the tell on three sides, the best place to see Mesha's re-fortification is on the more gently sloping north east corner where huge stones compose a formidable corner wall. David's men began his census here thus pointing to Israelite occupation (2 Samuel 24:5). It was originally part of the inheritance of Reuben (Joshua 13:16) but was in fact re-fortified by the Gadites (Numbers 32:34). It represented the southernmost place controlled by the Arameans (2 Kings 10:33) and when last mentioned in the Bible it was back in Moabite control (Jeremiah 48:19).

Left: These stones mark the re-fortification that took place under the Moabites. Behind, you can see the Wadi Arnon

Lehun

Lehun is another multi-period gateway city in a dramatic and beautiful location guarding the main crossing points over the Arnon Gorge. Although the numbering system has worn away, there are helpful plaques to guide the visitor round the site. The main Moabite section can be seen nearest to the Arnon Gorge. The central north gateway of the Moabite fortress is partly the work of restoration, but components such as its huge lintel are clearly original. There are four interior corner towers, a large courtyard and casemate walls (to be seen on the south and west of the fortress). In times of conflict these rooms on the wall could be filled in to give extra protection. It is thought to have been a storage fortress for nearby biblical Aroer. There is a museum here, as well as an earlier Bronze Age settlement and a small Nabataean temple dating to roughly the time of Christ.

Umm-er Resas

Umm er-Resas is the most likely site of biblical Mephaath, a levitical city on the edge of the desert known for its pasture land (Joshua 21:37) and described as being on the tableland (Jeremiah 48:21). Its name was preserved in the Roman era when it was known as Kastron Mephath pointing to it being a Roman military camp at that time. It is a world heritage site noteworthy for a superb mosaic representing nearly thirty Middle Eastern cities—a kind of panorama and celebration of nearby Christendom at the time. Whereas the Madaba mosaic map (see page 50) illustrated biblical sites, the Umm er-Resas mosaic illustrated the extent of the Christian

Above: The restored gate of the Moabite fortress at Lehun. Like that of Aroer it overlooks the Arnon

Right: The monk's tower at Umm er-Resas. The second building may have been a guest house for those coming to consult the holy man

world of the 8th century. On the main mosaic are eight towns from Israel (Jerusalem, Nablus, Sebastia, Caesarea, Lyd, Beit Gibrin, Ashkelon, Gaza), seven from Jordan (Umm er-Resas, Amman, Madaba, Hesban, Ma'in, Rabbah, Kerak) ten cities from the Nile Delta, and a couple more villages in Jordan called Limbon (possibly Libb at the turning point for Macchaerus) and Diblaton (probably biblical Beth-Diblathaim—see Jeremiah 48:22).

There are a number of other partially restored churches at the site, as well as domestic dwellings. The walls of the Roman fortress are still standing and can be traced. Names in church mosaic inscriptions confirm the Arab-Christian identity of the town. The 15m (49ft) high tower, a kilometre from the main town, is thought to have been used by a solitary monk, on the pattern of Simeon Stylites near Aleppo in the 5th century AD. Crosses on the sides of the tower, plus its location would support this identification. The adjacent church has been dated to the 6th century giving a possible similar date for the tower. Next to the tower is a possible guest house for visitors. Nearby is a cistern and a quarry.

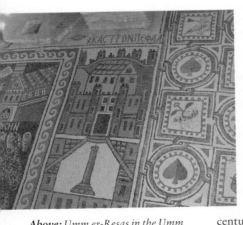

Above: Umm er-Resas in the Umm er-Resas mosaic; the pillar is not the monk's tower but another structure with a cross on top. Notice the defacement of parts of the surrounding mosaics which took place during the one hundred year struggle in the Orthodox Church over the legitimacy of 'icons' (of which mosaics are one form)

Khirbet Mudayna-Thamad

Mudayna-Thamad may be the best place in Jordan to see a significant Moabite city. As well as the beauty of the site within the curve of a stream bed full of oleander trees, it is a very full Moabite city with a six-chambered gate as its most impressive feature. At the end of this gate complex, on the left, is a small Moabite temple. Next to, and in front of, the gate are the remains of a tower and a multi-god worship shrine for travellers. The stones were there to represent any god. There are textile and food production rooms in and behind the gate complex. In the furthest excavated area from the gate, a casemate wall can be found. There are Nabatean/Roman remains on the level area before you get to the tell.

Ruth and her family could have come from a city like this. Mudayna-Thamad may well be biblical Jahaz: 'Sihon would not allow Israel to pass through his territory. He gathered all his people together and went out against Israel to the wilderness and came to Jahaz and fought against Israel.' (Numbers 21:23)

Dead Sea Panorama

The Dead Sea Panorama complex includes a superb look-out point over the Dead Sea and the Judaean hills and a large hall dedicated to putting the Dead Sea in context. A number of panels illustrate its geology, flora, fauna and history. There are also examples of the area's rocks and a graphic model of the sea level decline.

Top: *Six chambered gate at Mudaynah-Thamad*

Above: *The entry shrine at Mudaynah. It is thought that it was suitable for any god. Notice the standing (sacred) stones*

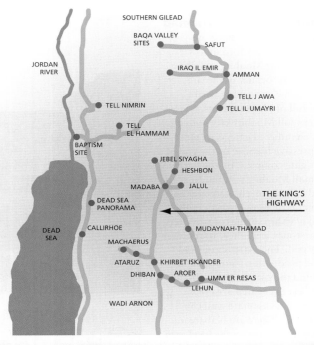

SOUTHERN GILEAD

TRAVEL INFORMATION

Madaba

The road to Madaba is signposted from Seventh Circle. Take the airport road and follow the signs. Madaba has a number of restaurants including Haaret Jadudna which is situated in an attractive restored Ottoman house. As Madaba is a quieter environment than Amman, some people choose to stay in Madaba instead. Once in Madaba a brown sign will direct you to **Mount Nebo.** It is 10km west of Madaba.

For **Machaerus** carry on south along the main road straight through Madaba until you get to the village of Libb where a sign will point right, off the main road to Mukawwir (local name for Machaerus). Follow this road as far as it goes. **Ataruz i**s on the same road as for Machaerus. After the turn-off from the main King's Highway proceed for 12.8km as if going to Machaerus and it is on your left.

Return to the main road and continue south to reach **Dhiban** and the **Wadi Arnon (Mujib)**.

Khirbet Iskander is just off the main road from Madaba to Dhiban where the road crosses Wadi Wala. Turn right before it goes over the river from the north.
Aroer Go through Dhiban and towards the end of the city you will see an intersection, take the road to the left signposted Umm er-Resas. Follow this road for a few kilometres and you will see a sign for Ara'ir (not Aroer) which is a turn-off on the right. Follow this for a few kilometres and you will see the tell which is on Wadi Mujib directly. It is

not a big site. Return to the road from which you were signposted to Aroer and go east for a couple of kilometres and you will see a sign for Lehun. It is a faded square blue sign. Turn right and you will come to **Lehun village** and the site after a couple of kilometres. Return to the road from which you were signposted to Lehun and continue on to Umm er-Resas.

An alternative route to **Umm er-Resas** is along the desert highway from Amman which you should continue on for about an hour; when you come to three tall antennae on the left you should turn right along a signposted road to Umm er-Resas.

Khirbet Mudaynah-Thamad

As you are coming out of Madaba on the main road south, take the turn-off left for Umm er-Resas at the traffic lights. After around 10km you will need to turn right at what looks like a T-junction. After roughly a further 9 km, turn left for Jiza (marked by a blue sign). Follow this minor road to Jiza for just under 2km and then turn left. Follow this track for just over 2km when you turn right down another track. You will see the tell just beyond an encampment of corrugated iron dwellings. Park above the wadi (valley) that separates you from the tell.

Dead Sea Panorama

Signposted from the Dead Sea road after the hotels or take the southwest road to Ma'in from Madaba. The complex includes a restaurant.

There are buses to Madaba from Tababor, Mahatta and Wihdat bus stations. From Madaba there are buses to Mukawir and Dhiban but most of the other sites are a little harder to get to by public transport. There is no direct bus to and from Mount Nebo although the infrequent bus from Madaba to South Shuneh goes past.

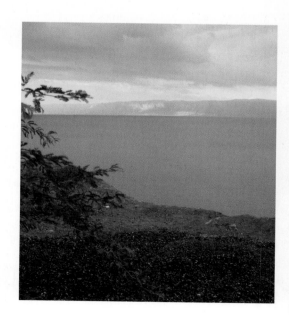

Right: *View of the Dead Sea*

⑤ Ruth's Moab

Although some of the best sites for the Moabite history are probably north of Wadi Arnon, that area was not their homeland. In going south over the Arnon we now enter the Moabite heartland

Callirhoe

Next to the modern main road going along the Dead Sea and near a major hot spring source, Callirhoe was the port of Herod the Great on the Dead Sea and seems to have included what is called his 'bath palace'. In Herod's day the sea would have been much higher and therefore today the wall lines of his harbour are some distance from the water. These wall lines, carved passages in the bedrock, and some columns confirm that this was indeed a significant settlement on the shore of the Dead Sea. Although a few kilometres apart, it is probable that Callirhoe and Machaerus were, as it were, one community. Across the main Dead Sea road, a little up the hill and directly opposite the port, are some more ruins; the structure with the deep cistern-type pool may have been part of Herod's bath palace as some design comparisons have been noted with a Herodian palace in Jericho.

Bab edh-Dhra

The name means 'gate of the arm' in Arabic and, taken together with the Early Bronze Age cemetery on the opposite side of the road,

is a huge site especially for the Dead Sea region. It towers 180m (550 feet) above the surface of the Dead Sea, now some way away. The walled city contained 4.9 hectares (12 acres) of land and was occupied for over a thousand years. The site is difficult to interpret although walls, some of which were originally 7m (21ft) wide, are visible today. At the south-west end, inside the walled city, some kind of Canaanite temple has been identified. The city was destroyed in the 3rd millennium BC but there was a

Above: The highland of Moab was fertile and suitable for agriculture and also sheep raising

Facing page: The Dead Sea that formed the border for Moab

second occupation which ended before Abraham's time.

There are reckoned to have been twenty thousand tombs in the massive cemetery opposite the main site. It appears to have been a burial ground for the surrounding area and not just for Bab edh-Dhra. Numeira, a sister city, did not have a cemetery. There were round shaft tombs which went straight down into the ground and there were also what are known as charnel houses; round or rectangular structures partly above ground for multiple re-burials, in addition to simple mound graves. (See Box on page 108: Sodom and Gomorrah).

Above: Part of Herod's port on the Dead Sea

Below: Part of wall at Bab edh-Dhra

Numeira

Archaeologists have concluded that a whole section of the town of Numeira has crumbled away, thus we cannot get an idea of its size from the remains on its summit. There was a 7.5m (23ft) wide defensive tower. The defensive wall was 3m thick (10ft). It was between a quarter to half a hectare in size and a

stream provided water for the town. There are indications that the town was abandoned, perhaps because of the warnings of an earthquake, evidenced by the fact that doorways had deliberately been made secure. A few inhabitants remained and their skeletons were found; they may have been incinerated in the fires

Who were the Moabites?

The Moabites, like the Ammonites, were the descendants of Abraham's nephew Lot (Genesis 19:37). Their heartland was the whole area between the Wadi Arnon and the Wadi Zered but their kingdom for a time also occupied the area north of the Wadi Arnon, and south of the Ammonite kingdom, roughly defined by a line running east of the north end of the Dead Sea. Their national god was Chemosh, who was mentioned twelve times in the Moabite Stone (once in compound form with Ashtaroth) and also in Scripture, as one of the 'gods' that snared Solomon (1 Kings 11:7). However, some believe Chemosh may have been a regional deity as well. The Moabites' land was not to be encroached on (Deuteronomy 2:9) and yet they were to be excluded from the Israel assembly (Deuteronomy 23:3). Often, however, the relationship between the two peoples was antagonistic. The Moabite king, Balaak, called on Balaam to curse Israel (Numbers 22 to 24) and the Moabites, with the Midianites, led the people of Israel astray (Numbers 25). Eglon, king of Moab, subjugated Israel for eighteen years (Judges 3:14).

Nonetheless Ruth the Moabitess has a whole book centred round her and appears in the genealogy of Christ (Matthew 1:5). It seems that the Moabite and Hebrew languages were sufficiently close for communication between Ruth and her successive Israelite husbands not to be a problem. In the Iron Age there was continued fighting between the two peoples. The Moabites were attacked by the prophets for, among other things, their pride (Isaiah 16:6). By paying tribute, the Moabites flourished under the Assyrian empire but were subjugated by the Babylonians. They did not appear as a separate province under the Persians, but were mentioned by Josephus in the Hellenistic era. Modern discoveries, including the uncovering of two Moabite temples, have increased our knowledge of their life and religion.

Above: One of the ways up into Moab was Luhith, probably Wadi I'sal shown here

that followed the earthquake—if that is what triggered the conflagration that ended the town's existence. A complete bunch of grapes 4,000 years old was found in one room beside a sickle! Opposite the site of Numeira is a Nabatean fortress.

Dayr Ayn Abata—Lot's cave

Perched on a steep cliff near the modern town of Ghor Safi is a clutch of monastic buildings built around a cave that had its first use over 5,000 years ago. The site of this settlement agrees with the

Above: Part of the fortification of
Numeira by the Dead Sea

Left: 'Lot's pillar' by the Dead Sea

Below: The Byzantines built a church
around the cave in which they believed
Lot and his daughters took refuge

location given it by the Madaba
map. With regard to the location
of Sodom (see Box: Sodom and
Gomorrah on page 108), all we
can say is that the early church
celebrated the cave as the one
where Lot took refuge. The cave

itself had a white
mosaic floor and then a
second chamber whose
floor was covered in
marble. The monastic
water system and
reservoir is interesting,
as is the fact that the
main church is built
round the entrance to
the cave. One of the
mosaics discovered
has an inscription in

cross wishing us 'a good end'.
ear the site is a spring which is
ill home to two kinds of fish,
nails and aquatic plants. A
useum should be open by 2010
elow the site of this Byzantine
onastic complex which provides
ood views over the southern end
f the Dead Sea and is well worth
visit whatever one's opinion is
n the location of Sodom.

alu'

s dramatic position on a
ibutary wadi leading on to the
rnon helps make up for the
asalt chaos that greets you as
ou enter the sprawling city of
alu'. Geologically situated on the
va outflow from nearby Jebel
hihan, Balu' is the largest city in
Moab and may well have been Ar
Numbers 21:15). It is around 550
y 300m (373 by 187 yds) in size.

Further to the east a courtyard
ouse on the casemate wall
as excavated which included
possible cultic room because
f the discovery in it of a sacred
one and a female figurine. The
ntels of the house are still in
lace. There has been excavation
f other structures including some
front of the castle.

ebel Shihan

ebel Shihan, an extinct volcano,
ominates the northern Moab
ea and from it there are
veeping views in all directions.
nce a military post, the summit
nd its slopes are now accessible
y car to visitors although you
ill need to walk the last section.
here are wall lines, columns
nd pottery from the Bronze Age
nwards. There is an ancient

*Above: The castle at Balu' is the most
prominent building and is almost
certainly Moabite in origin*

*Above: The famous Balu' stela,
whose inscription is tantalisingly
indecipherable, is in the Amman
museum; the Egyptian-style stele
seems to depict the local king being
given authority by a god and a
goddess. © DoA. Jordan*

Above: Jebel Shihan towers above Northern Moab

Bottom: The ruins of the Qasr Temple

Inset: The sun god found at Qasr emphasising the eclectic nature of Nabataean worship

1.3m thick (4ft) wall around the ancient citadel on the summit and there are the remains of towers on the south-west and possibly the south-east, and a possible gateway on the western wall. A cistern and a 5m (15ft) diameter oval shaped pool have also been found. A column on the site may be a Roman milestone. A cistern and previously inhabited caves are found on the south side of the mountain near the summit and 400m (250yds) from the summit, to the southwest, are the remains of a black basalt building compound. Between this basalt compound and the summit is another structure including two rooms and a courtyard.

The biblical identification of Shihan is not clear, but it could possibly be connected with Sihon king of the Amorites.

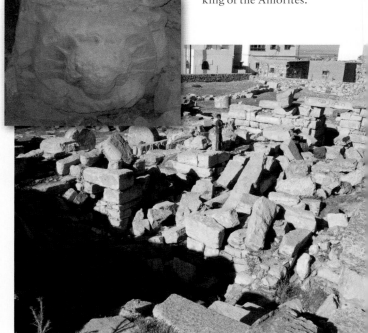

Qasr

Situated on the King's Highway, Qasr has a substantial Nabataean temple or at least a building used for religious purposes. It dates from the 2nd or 3rd century AD and has Nabataean features paralleling Qasr il bint at Petra and Dhiban, as well as Roman features. It is on an east-west axis with the entrance on the east. There are two towers flanking the entrance to the temple which, in total, covers an area of 32 by 27m (104 by 88ft). The probable sanctuary area at the back of the temple is divided into three sections. A staircase was also found. It would have been surrounded by a courtyard whose extent has been impossible to determine. A tunnel brought water to the cistern which is at the southern end of the courtyard and there are other cisterns and channels in the area of the temple. The stones were re-used and it seems that among the representations of gods from the temple at Qasr are those of the Graeco-Roman sun god Helios

Above: The Roman temple at Rabbah

Below: This impressive Crusader castle at Kerak dominates the surrounding area

and Lycurgos who was associated with Dionysius.

Rabbah

On the King's Highway between Qasr and Kerak is Rabbah, an important Roman city. Because of its central position in Moab it would have been a natural choice for the Moabite capital Ar (Numbers 21:28) although Balu' was the bigger city. Today

Kerak

Kerak is mentioned by its various names several times in the Old Testament: Isaiah 15:1, 16:7,11; Jeremiah 48:31,36 and 2 Kings 3:25–27. In addition to its commanding elevation, it is strategically located at a crossroads between the King's Highway and an east-west route from the desert to the Dead Sea. The name comes from the Aramaic 'Karka' ('the walled town'). A brief 6th or 7th century Moabite inscription found here mentions a Moabite king making an altar for the god Chemosh.

The crusader castle that dominates the skyline includes a church and is well worth a visit. In the castle museum there are useful displays of Moabite and other artefacts from the region and a case showing the kind of remains that were discovered in a typical Bab ed-Dhra tomb. The explanatory plaques in English contain helpful summaries of Moabite and other historical periods.

Top: View of Wadi Zered from Khirbet Tannur

Above: View of Khirbet Tannur with temple area on the right

a fenced-off area next to the main road contains a Roman street, a partially re-used Roman temple dating approximately to the time of the universal persecution of the Church in the early 4th century and a Byzantine church. Nearby is an ancient reservoir dating back at least to the Roman era.

Khirbet Tannur

Atop this forbidding hill, standing on the edge of biblical Wadi Zered and next to the King's Highway, was a significant Nabatean temple with dimensions of 48 by 40m (157 by 131ft).

On the basis of 'once a holy site, always a holy site', an earlier Edomite worship structure may

ave preceded it here, although
o Edomite remains have been
ound. However, the site's only
ritten inscription mentions
ot a Nabataean god, but the
domite god Qos. To further
omplicate the religious scene,
 the sanctuary of the temple,
atues representing Dushara and
is female consort Uzza, were
ound in the form of the Syrian
od Zeus-Hadad (or Baal) and
tagartis! Another representation
f Atagartis from the site is in
he Amman citadel museum. It
 thought that these images of
oreign gods were worshipped
y the Nabateans as their own
ods. This careless mixture helps
s to appreciate God's stringent
arning to Israel that they had
nly one God and were not to
ingle his worship with false gods
Deuteronomy 4:15–20;7:5–6).

Dedicatory inscriptions of the
mple go back to roughly the
me of Christ, but parts go back
o the 1st century BC. It was built
 phases and destroyed by
n earthquake in the 4th
entury AD. The plan of the
mple included an outer
nd inner court and one
tar in the north-east area
f the outer court.

The views over the Wadi
ered are magnificent,
nd the Nabatean choice
f site, which contains no
her buildings, is best

appreciated by the ascent of the
summit—very possible for an
averagely fit person. Khirbet
Tannur may have been the
sanctuary in which Herod the
Great spent a night on his way to
Sinai, as recalled by Josephus.

Khirbet adh-Dharih

Khirbet adh-Dharih is an
attractively located site situated
among olive groves above Wadi
Laban, a tributary that flows into
Wadi Zered. The honey-coloured
Nabataean temple has been
excellently restored. Occupied by
the Edomites, among others, what
we see today are the remains of a
Nabataean settlement containing
a temple, village and associated
cemetery. The site was later
reoccupied in the Byzantine era
after its abandonment following
the earthquake of AD 363.

The temple had an open
air entrance area facing an
elaborately designed façade which
was 15m high (49ft). A main

*ight: The sanctuary at
hirbet adh-Dharih with the
rt of interior façade left in
ace by the archaeologists*

Above: The alcove for the image of
the god at Dhat Ras.

entrance led to the sanctuary
where a square platform built
over two crypts was surrounded
by a covered corridor and four
small rooms. The square holes
on the 7m (23ft) square altar
platform were for betyls (god

blocks) and the small round hole
were to let the blood from the
sacrifices drain away. A Byzantir
church was built in the temple
and the semi-circular foundation
of the apse has been left in place.
The nearby village with a numbe
of small houses was higher up
and included four olive presses.
Excavations of the tombs to the
east of the village discovered
artefacts made of gold.

Dhat Ras

At Dhat Ras another Nabatean
temple has been dated
approximately to the time of
Christ. The temple is on a podiu
and has very thick 1.8m (6ft)
walls. It is not known which god'
image the niche in the sanctuary
of this temple contained. There
is another chamber above this
sanctuary, a so-called attic. Wha

Left: Part of the fort at Mudaybi, wit
the crucial desert corridor in evidenc
behind

is unusual about this temple is its subterranean cistern. It is thought that this may have been used for ritual washing or simply as an offering to the deity. The temple design facilitated water collection in this cistern which was not for normal domestic use.

On the hill on the edge of the city, precariously held in place by gravity, are the remains of another Nabataean structure looking rather lopsided and as if it is about to topple over.

Mudaybi

Mudaybi is an 84 by 89m (275 by 291ft) square Moabite fort which may have been abandoned due to an earthquake not long after it was built. Dating to the Iron Age, it may well have been built during the Assyrian period. Situated on a wadi that linked the King's Highway with the Desert Highway, it is thought that it was built to keep an eye on people coming from the desert to the fertile Kerak area. There is an impressive view of this desert passageway from the tell. The eastern wall contains a good four chambered gate measuring 15 by 20m (49 by 65ft) which was originally roofed with wood, mud and reeds. Huge stones were used in its construction, some measuring over 3m (10ft). On either side of the entrance were towers. There is also a bench and some pavement. Also originating in the gate complex were some column heads with spiral decoration. The excavators found the remains of fifty species of food plants, in addition to bones of fish thought to be from the Red Sea. Sixty-eight loom weights in the domestic area of the fort testify to cloth production. Excavations are ongoing and within the Moabite fort is a late Byzantine/ early Islamic structure.

Above: The fine four chamber gate at Mudaybi

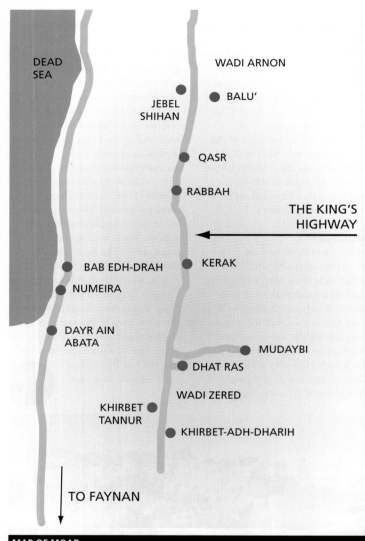

DEAD
SEA

WADI ARNON

JEBEL
SHIHAN

BALU'

QASR

RABBAH

THE KING'S
HIGHWAY

BAB EDH-DRAH

KERAK

NUMEIRA

DAYR AIN
ABATA

MUDAYBI

DHAT RAS

WADI ZERED

KHIRBET
TANNUR

KHIRBET-ADH-DHARIH

TO FAYNAN

MAP OF MOAB

TRAVEL INFORMATION

Apart from **Kerak**, for which you should take a bus from Amman's Wihdat bus station, the sites in Moab are best accessed by car. In Kerak, there is a restaurant next to the castle.

You can see **Callirhoe** from the road but it is 18.5km past the first checkpoint (just before you get to the hotels) on the road running alongside the Dead Sea.

For the sites of **Bab Ed-Dhra, Numeira** and **Dayr Ain Abata** the visitor can take the Dead Sea road from Amman down the eastern side of the Sea and at the junction with the turn-off for Kerak you will find **Bab ed-Dhra** about 0.5km up the road. **Numeira** is around 8.5km further south from the turn-off for Kerak. Look out for a Nabataean fort on your right because Numeira is opposite it. The exit for Lot's cave is roughly 22km south of the Kerak turn-off. The **Faynan** turnoff is roughly 81km south of the Kerak turn-off.

For **Balu'** cross the Wadi Arnon and, at the second village on the King's Highway after the gorge, turn left where you see a big gold-coloured coffee pot by the road. After 0.5km turn right at the mosque and follow this winding road which soon starts going across country and for a time you will need to keep an orchard on your right. After 3km on this road turn left and follow a rougher track for 1k that goes across a shallow wadi and takes you to the site.

For **Jebel Shihan** the road that takes you most of the way up the mountain is next to the tall antenna on the main King's Highway shortly

past the Balu turnoff. **Qasr** and **Rabbah** are further down the King's Highway before Kerak. Both **Khirbet Tannur** and **Khirbet adh-Dharih** are signposted from the King's Highway in, and just as you come out of, the Wadi Zered (or Hasa)

Dhat Ras is signposted from the King's Highway after Mazar. For **Mudaybi** take the turn-off from the King's Highway south of Mazar that is signposted Al abyad and Muhay. Go to the outskirts of the village of Um Hamat which is around 7.5km from this turn-off. Follow the main road, but there

is one roundabout where you need to bear left. If necessary ask for the village of Um Hamat. On the edge of the village of Um Hamat is a Y-junction, the left fork of which goes into the main village. Take the right fork and go east across country for 8.4km (after 0.35km you will pass a mosque and mini-market on your left.) The road gets rougher and rougher but is do-able in an ordinary car provided it is dry. The fort uses black rocks.

For more information on Mudaybi go to www.vkrp.org

Above: The Rujm al'Abd stele, which is a possible depiction of the Moabite god Chemosh, was found in the area of Jebel Shihan and is now in the Louvre Museum in Paris. © Mark Connally

⑥ Edom—Esau's land

Edom was the highest and the driest of the three kingdoms across the river and, unlike those of the Moabites and the Ammonites, it eventually extended over the other side of the Rift Valley

Wadi Zered

Wadi Zered starts in the eastern desert and runs into Safi and the Dead Sea. It is 56km (35mi) long and between 5.6km (3.5mi) and 6.4km (4mi) wide. It is shallower than the Arnon gorge, but separated the two peoples of Edom and Moab and is mentioned in Deuteronomy 2. In Numbers 21:12, the people of Israel encamped in the wadi itself. There are a number of sites in and above Wadi Zered, including Khirbet Tannur.

Sela

Sela, which is near Tafila and Buseirah, may well be the place of the same name where 10,000 Edomites were cast down by Amaziah (2 Chronicles 25:12). It is also the same word in Arabic as 'cliff'. It seems to be an archetypal Edomite 'acro-site' (a site on the pinnacle of a mountain) which made it difficult to access. A carved inscription, from the Babylonian period unique to Jordan, can just be made out from opposite the site. It records the victories of Nabonidus, the father of Belshazzar (Daniel 5:1), and would date his attack on Edom to 551 BC. Unfortunately most

of the text is worn away. As well as the figure of Nabodinus there are symbols of the sun and moon, recalling Job's protestation in Job 31:26–28.

Sela consists of a narrow way up the mount with a carved gateway as the only entrance, a reservoir with square opening, cisterns and a high place on the south of the mount. It seems that the cisterns on the summit are Edomite, rather than Nabatean, confirming Sela as an Edomite stronghold. Edomite pottery has also been found there. There is an

Above: *A tributary, Wadi Laban, flowing into Wadi Zered*

Facing page: *Camels travelling through the incomparable scenery of Wadi Rum where there is evidence of Nabataean rather than Edomite occupation*

isolated rock on the summit with twelve steps leading nowhere, which could be Edomite. However, much of what can be seen on the summit is Nabataean and there is a Nabataean dam and water system in the outer rock outcrop before you get to the area in front of the narrow way up the mountain.

Left: Sela

Right: The Nabonidus inscription from Sela. © Mark Connally

Who were the Edomites?

The Edomites were descended from Esau, twin brother of Jacob (Genesis 36). Israel was to regard Edom as a brother (Deuteronomy 2:4,8 and 23:7–8) and respect their land. Later, however, David conquered the Edomites (2 Samuel 8:14) and, as predicted, Jacob came to rule over Esau. The Edomites rebelled (2 Chronicles 21:8) and later came under severe judgement for their attitude towards Israel's fall (Obadiah 8–14). Daniel 11:41 gave them some hope, but judgement on Edom is the dominant theme throughout the Bible (Malachi 1:2–4). The Amalekites, Israel's bitter enemies (1 Samuel 15:1–3) were an Edomite sub-group.

The Edomites did not languish under Assyrian rule, but they were subjugated by the Babylonians under Nabonidus. There is some evidence for their presence in the Persian period. Their heartland was between Wadi Zered and Wadi Hisma (near Aqaba), but they spread further south and later moved into parts of southern Judah.

Knowledge of Edomite religious life has been helped by the discovery of two Edomite religious shrines in the Negev where they also settled. Their god was Qos (meaning 'bow' in Arabic) but even so, little is known of their precise beliefs. Their language was largely indistinguishable from Hebrew.

Their dwelling 'in the clefts of the rocks, in lofty dwellings' (Obadiah 3) is an accurate description, and some of their highland settlements are still hard to access today. Recent excavations have focussed on lowland sites associated with the Edomite copper mining industry and these give support to their being an effective power at the time of David. Edom later became Idumaea, which was the homeland of Herod the Great; he was half Edomite. Later Idumeans heard Jesus (Mark 3:8).

Buseirah

Buseirah is the biblical Bozra, mentioned around seven times in the Old Testament mainly in the context of judgement against Edom (Jeremiah 49:13, 22; Amos 1:12). This Edomite capital city is the largest Edomite settlement yet discovered and almost certainly their royal city. Apart from some possible 10th or 9th century BC pottery found there, the main structures discovered at the site so far do not go back earlier than the 8th century BC. Up till now there has been no archaeological evidence that Buseirah was the capital of the kingdom that refused entry to the Israelites at the time of the conquest (Numbers 20:14–21). But it is in a strategic position being near the King's Highway and straddling an important west-east route. It was thought to guard the road through which traffic associated with the copper mining trade passed. A nearby spring, until recently also used by the modern village, was probably its main water source. Some public buildings were found on the tell, protected by a casemate wall. Next to the school, with most of it covered over, was a large public building with thick walls (up to 5m/16ft) which included a bathroom, part of which can be seen today. On the highest point of the site were two buildings, the smaller of which was built over the southern part of the lower building. There are design features in these buildings associated with the design of Assyrian temples. The upper building had a central courtyard and a number of rooms including a large reception room on the south-west. To the west of the main buildings there is a gateway to the acropolis.

Shawbak

At 1,412m (4,630ft) above sea level, Shawbak castle is one of

Top: The ideal location of Edom's capital city Bozrah (Buseirah) at the end of a neck of land protected on most sides

Above: Part of the superimposed public buildings on the Buseirah acropolis

Right: Shawbak castle

the highest points in Jordan and lies at a strategic point in the Edomite highlands. Originally a 12th century Crusader castle, the Muslims built a palace complex here. However the remains of a church and a chapel can still be seen and its striking location and substantial remains make it worth visiting.

Udruh

Udruh was a large oasis and Nabataean town at the time of Christ. 2.5 tons of Nabataean pottery were found at the kiln just outside the present Roman fort. A staging post between Arabia and the Mediterranean, when the Romans took over Nabataea in AD 106 a significant Roman fort was built here with four corner towers and twenty-four interval towers. It is approximately 250

by 200m (820 by 656ft) in size and the walls were 6m in height and contain a Byzantine church. At Tell Udruh to the south-east of the fort there was an Edomite settlement and, on top of that, Nabataean remains. There is a massive limestone quarry in the immediate vicinity of Udruh.

Khirbet Nahas

Khirbet Nahas is the site of an important Edomite copper smelting complex. The 10 hectare (25 acre) site is the biggest copper smelting site in southern Levant and there are reckoned to be tens of thousands of tons of copper slag strewn around. The slag heaps are several metres high. It also included one of the largest Iron Age fortresses in the area, dated by radio-carbon techniques to the 10th century BC. The fortress included a four chamber gate and a bench inside the central passage. Opposite the fortress on the other end of the tell is a well-excavated Edomite house. There are dozens of Edomite buildings on the tell. As an introduction to the copper smelting industry that took place in the area and the effect it had on the landscape, Khirbet Nahas is a good place to start.

Above: A gate at the fort of Udruh

Left: The back view of Khirbet Nahas largely built on copper slag. Notice the structures on the mound

Below left: General view of Faynan area south of Khirbet Nahas with acacia trees

Bottom left: Wadi Faynan at sunset

hirbet Faynan

hirbet Faynan, one of the ost important copper mining nd smelting sites in the area, ortunately also today boasts n eco-lodge and a small village earby. It is biblical Punon entioned in Genesis 36:41 and Jumbers 33:42–43, one of the stopping places of the people of Israel on their way to the land of Canaan. Because of it being at the centre of such an important copper production area, Khirbet Faynan would have had a number of trade routes passing through it. There are many mines in the immediate vicinity and also huge quantities of copper slag.

Khirbet Faynan is also infamous as a site of the martyrdom of Christians in the cruel persecution by the Roman emperor Diocletian in the early 4th century. Eusebius wrote in his history of the church: 'But among the martyrs at Palestine, Silvanus, bishop of the churches about Gaza, was beheaded with thirty-nine others at the copper mines of Phoeno.' Life would inevitably have been short for those mining copper in the Faynan area, not least because the heat in summer can be oppressive. There are two churches and a monastic building at Khirbet Faynan commemorating the Christians who died there, as well as dozens of Christian tombs dating back to the Byzantine era.

Copper mining and smelting

The remains in the Faynan area are reckoned to constitute the finest industrial archaeology site in the world; the beginning of exploitation of the copper seams here has been dated to roughly 7,000 years before Christ. The area of copper-rich territory is roughly 500 sq. kilometres (over 300 sq. miles). During the Iron Age, the Faynan region seems to have overtaken Cyprus in copper production in the southern Mediterranean region. Many mines and smelting centres have been discovered and the evidence is of prehistoric industrial pollution on a criminal scale! Two of the biggest copper production centres were at Khirbet Nahas and Khirbet Faynan

Above: Copper slag from the smelting activity in the Faynan area

(see page 81). Modern techniques have made it possible to trace the provenance of copper used in artefacts. Such was the intensity of exploitation before Christ that one expert suggests that by the time the Romans came along they had to settle for lower grade copper.

In the last decade or so extensive excavation has taken place in the Faynan area and, as a result, strong indications of the existence of a viable Edomite kingdom going back to the 10th century and earlier have been discovered—something that had been questioned previously, partly as a result of the relative lack of sites in the Edomite Highland areas. As a result of these discoveries it is harder to accept a late date for the Edomite kingdom on archaeological grounds. Indeed copper may have played a far more important role in the economic life of Edom than hitherto realised.

Humayma

Humayma was an important Nabataean-Roman desert town. It is in a beautiful location in gently undulating desert surrounded by mountains on all sides, although at first glance the site itself is unappealing. According to a 6th century AD account, based on one from the 4th century AD, the Nabatean king Aretas III founded it in response to a vision he had when investigating the oracle in the area. He understood he was to seek a white place to found his city. Humayma was in fact on the main road from Aqaba to Petra—the only significant settlement between them—being 80km equidistant from each. It was the main city in the Hisma, the desert area south of the main Edomite plateau.

Humayma is an example of the Nabataean genius for water engineering in that some of the

Right: *Part of the irrigation system at Humayma*

water for this rather exposed site was brought in covered channels from springs nearly 30km to the north. Because of its location next to sandstone hills, it was also in a kind of flood plain and therefore able to take advantage of rain when it did come. The population of Humayma, during the Nabataean period of its existence (from around fifty years before Christ to a hundred years after), is reckoned to have reached 00 people. Strategically, the site would not have been particularly easy to defend and so, when the Romans annexed the Nabatean kingdom in AD 106, it was one of the two primary forts (the other was at Bosra in Syria) built to control the south and the associated incense routes.

The Humayma fort included headquarters building, commander's residence (or praetorium, see Matthew 27:27), granary and its own internal reservoir. The fort would have held a garrison of 500 soldiers. latrines, drains and pressurised water pipes have been found. An interesting feature of the fort is the external projecting towers as opposed to the more normal internal towers. To the south-east of the fort is a rectangular shrine. The patron god of Humayma seems to have been called Hawara (one of the names of Humayma), but the Romans had Jupiter Ammon as their patron god. So the shrine had two gods, Hawara and Jupiter. It was also at Humayma that a joint inscription to Jupiter and an unknown saviour god was found recalling Paul's experience in Athens (Acts 17:23).

Further south-east are the Roman baths where some of the tiling can still be seen. There are a number of cisterns and reservoirs at the site, and a good length of Roman road further to the north and some Islamic buildings opposite the visitor centre. To the west of the visitor centre are the foundations of a nicely restored church. Above this church is a smaller one and behind that are some Nabataean water channels and cisterns. Although the first

Left: A Roman shrine at Humayma wher[e] both a Roman an[d] a Nabataean god were worshippe[d]

churches at Humayma date from the early 5th century, it is thought that there may well have been Christians here from the 3rd century onwards at the latest. It has also been reckoned that in the Byzantine era the city had seven churches for a population of between 600 and 700 people. John Oleson, the main excavator of the site, reckons that by AD 700 the Christians had either converted to Islam or left. The Abbasids who took over the Islamic Empire from the Umayyads started out from here.

Wadi Rum

Wadi Rum with its ever-varied rock formations rising out of a desert 'sea' is also one of the heartlands of the Bedouin and on[e] of the most accessible places to get a 'feel' for the beautiful, but a[t] times harsh, reality of the desert. While a three hour trip in the bac[k] of a four wheel drive vehicle may be good for appreciating a sweep of scenery, it is probably best to spend some time alone soaking i[n] the silence. A walk of an hour or two can take the visitor to some places that are at the same time

Below: View of the desert sea of Wadi Rum

almost within sight of civilisation and yet often quiet enough, and far enough away from the village and the jeep trails, for relative solitude.

The Wadi Rum protected area (and the areas outside it) contains a number of sites, but these are often limited to early Arabic inscriptions and drawings or to the partial remains of Nabatean structures. Wadi Rum is near the biblical area of Midian, whose cultural significance has been confirmed by excavations further south in Saudi Arabia. Little datable material from the Old Testament era has been found in the Wadi Rum protected area itself, although clearly a mainly nomadic people are unlikely to leave much evidence behind them. It is probably best to see Wadi Rum as part of an area known to the sons of Ishmael from an early period.

Less than a kilometre from the modern village of Wadi Rum is a Nabatean temple from shortly after the time of Christ, which is dedicated to the Nabataean goddess Allat; it is built over a previous sanctuary dedicated to Lat whose dedication stone was incorporated into the new temple. The temple is 11 by 13m (36 by 42ft) with an interior shrine measuring 4 by 5m (13 by 16ft). It is based on the general principle of holy of holies surrounded by a colonnaded courtyard and is approached by steps. To the east of the temple is a building complex which includes a villa with a fine baths complex.

Above: *The Nabataean temple at Wadi Rum. Notice the altar in the centre*

To the west of the temple a path winds up into the mountain to the so-called 'Lawrence's Spring' (Ayn esh-Shallaleh) where there are a number of inscriptions and 'god niches' centred round the spring which was a Nabatean sanctuary. Aqueducts led from the spring to the temple area. One or two water channels can be seen at the spring, but the whole course of the Nabatean aqueducts can not be made out. T.E. Lawrence, who organised the Arabs against the Turks in the First World War, found this a refreshing place to come and sit, hence the name.

Aqaba

Aqaba is Jordan's only outlet to the Red Sea and it was up this inlet that Solomon's ships came delivering their rich goods (1 Kings 9:26–28). From Aqaba it is possible to see Saudi Arabia, Egypt and Israel. What makes an otherwise rather unpalatable stretch of sand attractive, are the mountains of these countries which offer an ever-changing panorama of colour against the backdrop of the sea. In the past, the port traded as far as Africa and India, and a number of land routes met there, including those to Syria, the Negev, Gaza and Sinai. Aqaba was a major copper trading entrance port. The Via Nova Traiana–the Roman road which replaced the super-highway known as the King's Highway– began here.

Somewhere in the vicinity of Aqaba were the two sites of Elath and Ezion-Geber (Deuteronomy 2:8). At one time Ezion-Geber was identified with Tell El-Kheleifeh, 500m (547 yds) from the sea. It is currently inaccessible for security reasons, but is due to be opened to tourists in the future as part of plans for the development of Aqaba. Even if Tell El-Kheleifeh is biblical Ezion-Geber, that still leaves the location of Elath unclear and some have identified Pharaoh's Island, 12km to the south of Aqaba, as Ezion-Geber. Pharaoh's Island, seen as the only natural port in the northern gulf of Aqaba, has a harbour facing the land and casemate walls.

What is claimed as Jordan's earliest purpose-built church is a rather sorry mud-brick spectacle. Glass from a cup used in church services was found in a chamber where it could be expected that ecclesiastical material would be stored. A piece of sandstone thought to be part of an offering table was also discovered. Some walls had multi-coloured painted plaster, but it was difficult to discern patterns. There was originally a flagstone floor. It may have been destroyed in the earthquake of AD 363, but was originally built at the beginning of the 4th century. Other indications of it having been a church are its eastward orientation and its general design.

Aqaba museum

The small Aqaba museum has a useful room devoted to discoveries from Humayma which include altars to Zeus and Jupiter, small chunks of Roman frescoes, fragments of marble chancel screens from a church, a Roman stop-cock and Nabataean material. There is also material from the temple at Wadi Rum and a Byzantine lintel that has the inscription 'May Jesus Christ triumph'. Ivories from the Islamic period are an interesting addition.

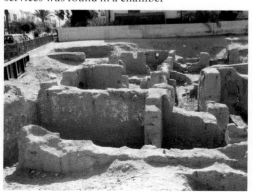

Left: General view of possibly the oldest purpose built church in world

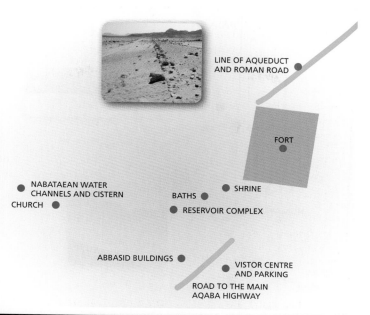

LINE OF AQUEDUCT
AND ROMAN ROAD

FORT

NABATAEAN WATER
CHANNELS AND CISTERN

CHURCH

BATHS ● ● SHRINE

● RESERVOIR COMPLEX

ABBASID BUILDINGS ●

● VISTOR CENTRE
AND PARKING

ROAD TO THE MAIN
AQABA HIGHWAY

MAP OF HUMAYMA

TRAVEL INFORMATION

Apart from **Aqaba**, the visitor really needs a car to see Edom. In Aqaba the church is opposite the JETT bus station and the museum is near the huge Jordanian flag. Several types of bus run from Amman to Aqaba, ranging from business class to the more basic (from Wihdat bus station).

Buseirah is signposted off the King's Highway. Go west down the main street of Buseirah as far as you can and you will come to a school, the last building on the plateau. The site is just beyond the school.

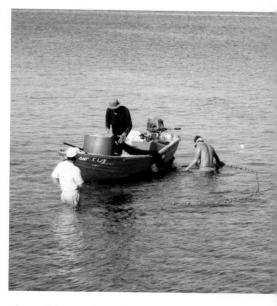

Above: Fishing in the Gulf of Aqaba

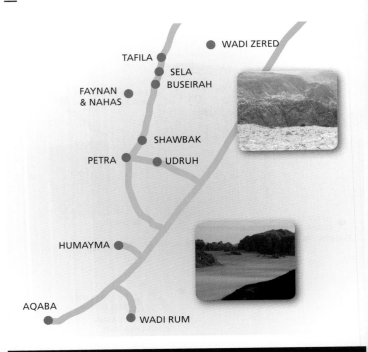

MAP OF EDOM

For **Sela,** take the turn-off from the King's Highway a few kilometres south of Tafila at the 'Sila Castle' sign. Go straight through the modern village of Ayn Bayda. The houses end and you start to descend into the gorge below. Continue on this winding road leaving the old village and visitor centre of Sela on your left and park in front of the big outcrop of rock at the bottom. Follow this outcrop on foot southwards, keeping it to your right and enter it where there is a wall built into the rock. Go west through this area.

Although the path is a little hard to follow you will see some modern steps in parts of the route and at the end you will need to turn sharp left down a gully which goes past an ancient Nabataean water system. This will take you to the open area in front of the rock of Sela itself, where you will see the modern steps which mark the start of the route up the rock.

Shawbak is on the way to Petra by the King's Highway. It is signposted and the turn-off is a little to the north of the town of Shawbak. **Udruh** is also close to Petra; you will see

the sign as you leave Petra to go to Amman.

Humayma is signposted from the main desert highway to Aqaba, not too many kilometres from where the road descends from the Ras IlNaqab ridge to the plain. Turn right at the corner of a tyre shop and go along the asphalted road till you reach the visitor centre. Google 'Robert Schick' and 'Humayma' for a good article on Christian Humayma on the Christus Rex website.

Wadi Rum is a turn-off to the left several kilometres further on. You can drive to Rum

village and then walk from there to the temple and Lawrence's Spring. For trips into the desert you can hire a pick-up at the entrance to the reserve where you pay your entrance fee. There are fixed routes and charges. Payment is by vehicle and not by the number of persons.

For the **Faynan** experience, it is actually possible to drive to Faynan in an ordinary vehicle but for **Khirbet Nahas** you need to negotiate with someone in the village of Quweira to drive you out there.

Above: Ba'ja, another inaccessible Edomite dwelling area near Petra

Below: Another copper production area was Khirbet Jaria seen in the distance here

❼ Petra—beauty and idolatry

Petra is a brilliant display of man's artistry in turning barren rock into a majestic wonder. This Nabataean capital represents the showcase of a civilisation that lasted for around eight hundred years and which, at its peak, was an influential part of the Near East

Although much of what we see in Petra today dates from the time of Christ, the Nabataeans were not an obviously biblical people (see Box: the Nabataeans on page 93). They flourished after the Old Testament period and are barely mentioned in the New Testament, so how can Petra help us to understand better the world of the Bible?

Their temples, like other temples of the Old Testament world, included a sanctuary which was made up of an entrance hall, a holy area and a holy of holies where an image of their 'god' was to be found. The sanctuary would be surrounded by a courtyard in which an altar would often be found (although it could be in the holy of holies). The Petra tombs are spectacular.

Isaiah was sent to condemn Shebna, a senior civil servant at the time of King Hezekiah, for building a tomb for himself (Isaiah 22:15–16). For Petra's elite, it seemed to be essential to leave an impressive burial behind them. It appears that the Nabataeans also had memorial meals for their dead, hence the proximity of dining places (triclinia) to some of the tombs. Paul's spirit 'was provoked within him' at Athens at the numerous gods (Acts 17:16); what would he have felt at Petra with the large number of god-representations, especially in the Siq (gorge)?

The Nabataeans largely avoided human and animal representations of their gods but later this practice crept in. If we look at its temples, processional

Above: *The palace tomb, one of the most impressive of those in the royal tomb area of Petra*

Facing page: *A view of Petra's main street. Much of the area in the foreground, which includes a view of part of the altar, would have been taken up with the courtyard to the Qasr el-Bint*

ways, its high places and its 'god-blocks' Petra opens a window on the thought world of paganism in Old Testament times that the prophets of Yahweh preached against. Later, when Petra became a Christian city it seems that the temples remained.

Path to the Siq and the Siq

The visit to Petra begins with the descent from the official entrance to the 'Siq' or gorge. On the way a number of what are essentially ornate tombs, including the square-shaped 'djin blocks', come into view. Djin is the Arabic for 'spirit'. Two prominent unrelated monuments on top of each other are the Obelisk Tomb and the Bab el-Siq Triclinium; both quite near the entrance to the Siq. This Triclinium was one of the places for having funeral meals for the dead.

The 1.6 km Siq with its thirty-five water inlets, seventy-one sacred niches and other monuments could easily be blocked. Some of its Nabataean paving can still be seen. Little of the original arch that marked its entrance can be seen today.

Khazneh

The Siq opens out onto a view of the Khazneh (treasury), justly Petra's most famous carving and best seen in the glow of the morning sun at around 10am or 11am. Of interest is the polytheistic nature of the façade. The Egyptian goddess Isis is centre stage below the orb at the top, although she could be a composite goddess for she appears to be carrying a cornucopia of the fruits of the earth (a symbol

Top right: Each 'betyl' (house of god, the same word as 'bethel') represented either a god or the god's dwelling place. Notice the platform for the god's dwelling

Right: Towards the end of the Siq on the left is this partially destroyed carving of a camel and camel driver. At one and a third life size it would have been one of the largest carvings in the area

of plenty) which is associated with the Greek goddess Tyche. At ground level are Castor and Pollux, who were the twin gods portrayed on the ship that carried Paul to Malta (Acts 28:11). The eagles hovering above the orb at the top are thought to represent the main Nabataean god, Dushara. Immediately below the Khazneh was another layer of tomb facades. The Khazneh is likely to have been a tomb, possibly for Aretas III. The interior seems to be set up for the offering of libations. In front of it was probably an artificial lake (as at Iraq Il Emir) thus making the overall spectacle even more impressive.

Outer Siq, Theatre and High Place of Sacrifice

The route continues past the Khazneh through a broader gorge (the outer siq), coming

Right: Aretas IV from a coin. © DoA. Jordan

Who were the Nabataeans?

Nebaioth was Ishmael's eldest son (Genesis 25:13). The identification of the Nabataeans with the descendants of Ishmael, while not universally accepted, is supported by some specialists and this would extend the Nabataeans' known history by a further twelve hundred years or so. A people called the 'Nabatu' is also mentioned in Assyrian texts of the 7th century BC.

The Nabataean kingdom, which bordered on Herodian Judaea flourished most spectacularly during the time of Christ. The mother of Herod the Great was Nabataean, as was the first wife of Herod Antipas, whom he left to take Herodias (Mark 6:17). The governor of Aretas IV was the cause of Paul's greatest humiliation (2 Corinthians 11:32–33)! Paul's 'Arabia' (Galatians 1:17) would have meant the Nabataean kingdom.

For 800 years the Nabataeans were a power in the area. As Arab nomads they were under a similar injunction to that given to the Rechabites in Jeremiah 35:6–7. According to a 1st century BC account, the Nabataeans were under an injunction—the infringement of which was a capital offence—not to sow seed, plant fruit trees, drink wine or build any house. Later they did build settlements, but eventually returned to their nomadic roots. For a period, they controlled the spice and aromatic trade from Arabia and from further afield. They were among the world's most skilled water engineers. Fiercely independent, their kingdom was taken over by the Romans in AD 106. Christianity reached the Nabataeans at an early period.

eventually, past more tombs to the Nabataean theatre that is carved out of the rock. It would have held 3,000–4,000 spectators and was constructed during the reign of Aretas IV (2 Corinthians 11:32)

Above: The Nabataeans were very eclectic in their gods and this is particularly evident in the Khazneh

Below: The small raised rectangular section in front of the altar was perhaps for non-liquid offerings and may have corresponded to the showbread offering of 2 Chronicles 2:4

A path on the left before the theatre, at the end of the Outer Siq, leads up to the High Place of Sacrifice. The round trip to the High Place, which can take anything from an hour and a half to three hours, should be a priority. The Petra high place is post-Old Testament, but it resembles older high places, quite possibly overlaying an earlier Edomite one. One of the best in the Middle East, among its points of interest are the central altar for animal sacrifices, the circular altar which was probably for drink offerings (or for washing the offerings before being offered) and a square projection in front of the altar for food offerings.

There is an open square-cut water tank 1.2m (4ft) deep to the south of the altar. There is also a sunken area in front of the altar which could have been surrounded by a wall as a way of marking it off as a cultic area in the midst of which could have stood a sacred stone. The whole carved area is extraordinarily well preserved. There is an alternative route down from the High Place—the Wadi Farasa route—going past several significant monuments and ending up in the colonnaded street.

Turning left down towards the Roman arch and colonnaded street, the way is opened to visit a Roman and three Nabataean temples.

An examination of their monuments and inscriptions reveal that the Nabataeans were polytheistic. Their main god was Dushara, followed by al-Uzza and the goddess Allat. They seem to have worshipped their gods under the guise of other deities like the Syrian goddess Atargatis. A majority of their worship objects are in non-human form (aniconic). One theory holds that 'Dushara' dwelt on Petra's highest peak, Jebel Haron, and that the various high places in the lower hills were all aligned with it. The various processional ways of the High Places reinforce their cultic nature. Some think that Dushara gave 'his name' to the Sharra mountains rather than the reverse. There seems to have been some sort of cult of the dead, with ritual banquets in the theatres and elsewhere, connected with belief in the continued existence of the dead. In Petra there are obelisks, or nephesh, standing for the souls of the dead, encapsulating their essence according to the thinking of the Nabataeans. The square shape of the betyls (see page 92) represented a fixed dwelling place for the gods.

The Great Temple

Although it is different in size and design from Herod's temple, the Great Temple is an excellent visual reminder that Herod's temple was a complex of buildings and courtyards rather than a rectangular building alone. The Great Temple covers a total area of 7,560 sq. m (24,803 sq. ft) or three quarters of a hectare. The area razed to take Herod's temple was around 13,500 sqm or 1.35 hectares. The Great Temple is made up of a triple colonnaded courtyard with hexagonal tiling in front of the sanctuary area. The upper courtyard area on the next level includes the large underground cistern with a capacity of nearly 400,000 litres (87,900 UK gallons or 105,670 US gallons), plaza areas, staircases, a temple forecourt area and the temple itself. It is not clear where the altar was, although small-horned incense altars have been found and a rectangular shape in

Above: A view of the Great Temple. The first steps lead up to the lower temenos and the second set of steps to the upper temenos and the main temple building

the lower courtyard area could have contained an altar. In front of the lower courtyard is the propylaeum, or ceremonial gate, which consists of stairs, rooms, galleries and some betyls.

Coming to the temple itself, it appears to have gone through several phases of building before reaching its present state. The actual temple or sanctuary area contains the unusual 600 seat theatre in place of the 'holy of holies'. The presence of this theatre has led some to doubt whether it was a temple, but the director of the Brown University Great Temple excavations, Martha Jukowsky, points out that rarely is sacred space made unsacred and she compares it to the secularisation of Herod's temple where all sorts of buying and selling took place (John 2:14).

There are a number of staircases, platforms and arches within the temple, as well as three interior chambers. Within the temple itself there are the remains of 2,000 year old paintwork on plaster in the corridors between its inner and outer walls. To the south of the main temple structure is a passageway where excavators found a carving of a god and a so-called chapel with a niche for a god. Egyptian, Indian and other influences have shaped the temple, for example the elephant heads on columns in the main courtyard.

Qasr el-Bint

For a long time Petra's only standing building was this major Nabataean temple dating to the time of Christ. The actual temple or sanctuary part of the complex is 32m by 32m (104ft by 104ft). Centrally located at a junction of routes, originally covered in white marble, it was typical of one of the two main kinds of Nabataean temples with a surrounding temenos (or courtyard area), a large exterior altar, an entrance area, sanctuary and an inner sanctuary. The latter was divided into three chambers, the central one of which would have contained a probable square representation of the deity. There was a double row of benches in the temenos which went up to the temple itself. The design of Qasr el-Bint is typical of many temples in the Old Testament period with all the main temple components organised on the same axis.

Temple of Winged Lions

This is another 1st century AD Nabataean temple, deriving its name from the presence of lions on the columns nearest the altar (which can no longer be seen). It is thought to be identified with the Syrian goddess Atagartis under her Nabataean name al-Uzza. The Temple of Winged Lions was originally approached by a road starting roughly at the temenos gate. It too, was surrounded by a colonnaded courtyard.

Above: *The temenos gate marks the beginning of the Qasr el-Bint temenos or courtyard area*

Right: The large altar in front of the Qasr el-Bint

In contrast to the Qasr el-Bint model, it represents the second kind of Nabataean temple design. Here there is an outer temple which encloses an entrance area, an inner temple and an inner sanctuary. In the sanctuary is a motab, or seat for the god, which is also an altar. Underneath the inner temple are various vaulted underground chambers.

Temple of the Imperial Cult

Built some time after the annexation of the Nabataean kingdom by Rome in AD 106 this small square temple would perhaps have been of more significance to Christians in Petra than the much grander and bigger Nabataean ones, since it could have been used either for worshipping the emperor as god or offering sacrifices for the well-being of the emperor (and by extension the Roman Empire of which Petra was now part). In certain places, at times during the early persecutions of the church, such sacrifices were mandatory. This temple is a little to the north of the Great Temple complex. Among the reasons which led to its identification as an Imperial Cult temple were its Roman design features, such as a podium with steps leading up to it, the

estimated four tons of marble used in its construction, and the inscriptions to the emperors found among its 624 inscriptions. The plan of this very small imperial temple is that of a portico or entrance area, a single chamber or sanctuary with two platforms and two square basins. It could have been up to 13m (41ft) high. A few original marble facing pieces have been left in place.

Petra Church, Blue Church and Ridge Church

On a hill next to the Temple of the Winged Lions and opposite the Great Temple are three churches. The largest of the three, covered by a protective shelter, is thought to have been Petra's cathedral.

Right: The altar in the Temple of the Winged Lions. Notice the marble flooring in front

Above: The small Imperial Cult temple

Right: On the other side of the courtyard in front of the main nave of the Petra Church is one of the finest baptistries in the Middle East which can be easily missed on a superficial visit

Below right: The Dayr (monastery) at Petra, similar in grandeur to the Khazneh and yet without any anthropomorphic carvings

The original church dates to the 5th century but it was remodelled in the 6th. As well as its tripartite apse, a very attractive fragment of chancel screen and a large nave (the central part of the church) can be seen. In the side chambers there are some fine mosaics, some of which appear secular in nature. It is also thought, on the basis of archaeological evidence, that the upper walls, arches and central apse were lined with mosaics. There is a courtyard in front of the church in which there is a well.

A little further up the slope is the Blue Church in which a pulpit was discovered, which was a visible reminder of the role of preaching in the early church. The bishop may have lived on the second floor of this church.

The topmost church is known as the Ridge Church. Based on an existing building, an apse and two other rooms were added in the 4th century. The church is built over a large cistern.

Petra scrolls

Discovered in Petra's main church in 1993, the 152 Petra scrolls represent the largest collection of ancient documents ever discovered in Jordan. Because they were carbonised and then covered in debris they survived a bad 6th century fire and have been painstakingly unravelled, transcribed, translated and put in historical context by an international team whose work is on-going.

They cover the period between AD 537 and 593 and include some of the longest papyri yet found from the ancient world. Although some of the names are Greek, others are clearly Nabataean and they thus present a partial picture of a flourishing—if somewhat prone to law suits—Christian Nabataean Petra at a time previously thought to be one of decline.

Their main protagonist was Theodorus who was a leader in the church, but a total of 350 people are mentioned including known historical figures. The scrolls deal with legal matters like inheritance and tax, change of a dowry arrangement and disputes between church members. They are a mine of information, not just on Petra, but also represent a source of pre-Islamic Arabic, albeit in Greek script.

Umm el-Biyyara

On one of Petra's highest peaks an Edomite settlement was discovered but, up to the present, there has been no evidence that it was a major Edomite centre as it seems only to have been inhabited for a few decades in the 7th century BC. Nonetheless the site is almost impregnable with only one way up (from the south-east). As well as a simple housing complex with low lintels, there are a number of cisterns from which the mountain gets its name and which are probably Edomite in origin. There is also a Nabataean temple on the summit. Halfway up the demanding climb is a Nabataean switchback ramp, some kind of processional way. The views from Um il Biyyara are some of the best in Petra but will cost the visitor a demanding climb of approximately one hour.

Dayr (monastery)

This hugely impressive façade with accompanying inner chamber is called the Dayr because of the evidence of Christian use (from the crosses inside) after the Nabataean period. In appearance it is very similar to the Khazneh, after which it appears to have

Above: The Blue Church gets its name from the fine blue marble columns, imported from Egypt, which adorn its structure

Left: Part of an Edomite housing complex on Umm il Biyyara

Middle: The Urn tomb is thought to have been a tomb of one of the Nabataean kings

Bottom: Inside the massive Urn tomb which became the original cathedral of Petra

from a red inscription that can still be seen today we know it was converted into a church in AD 447. It therefore has a double interest. Two recesses were joined together to make a kind of apse where the bishop's seat would have been. It was the original cathedral of Petra. There were also holes which would have been for the screen in front of the apse.

Jebel Khutba

The summit of Jebel Khutba contains another high place of sacrifice, shrines, a cistern and a processional way to its summit. It was clearly used for religious ceremonies. It is a shorter climb than the High Place of Sacrifice, although the latter is in a better state of preservation. Follow the royal tombs round the hill and you will come to the gated stairway which leads to the summit area. There are great views towards the public area of Petra and, on the south-west corner of the ridge, of the Khazneh. There was also an Edomite settlement on this hill.

been modelled, but without the human representations of the gods. It could have been used originally as a temple or a place for having feasts in honour of a departed king or, as some think, it could have had more than one use.

Urn tomb—another church

Thought to have been the tomb of one of the Nabataean kings;

Left: Part of the Jebel Khutba high place. The white square below is the Petra Church

Below: View from the il Khutba high place

Museums

Petra's main museum is next to the restaurant opposite Qasr il Bint, and the second museum overlooks it half way up the hill which holds the crusader fortress. Among the Edomite 'must-see' items in the main museum is the cuneiform tablet originally from Haran where Abraham lived for a time (Genesis 11:31). It was found at Tawilan near Petra and it records a transaction between Qaus-Shara, a local man and two Arameans. There are also Edomite and Nabataean incense burners and altars, thirty-six different oil lamps, many everyday objects such as bowls, jugs, keys, rings, needles and seals, Roman and Nabataean coins, and plenty of human and animal representations forbidden in Scripture. One or two items represent the Egyptian god 'bes', further emphasising the eclectic nature of Nabataean worship.

The smaller museum is halfway up the hill providing excellent views of the main street. It contains some Nabataean busts and carvings, and a case containing fragments of figurines. Edomite material, which is relatively rare in Jordan, includes an incense burner, a vessel for offerings to the gods and loom weights.

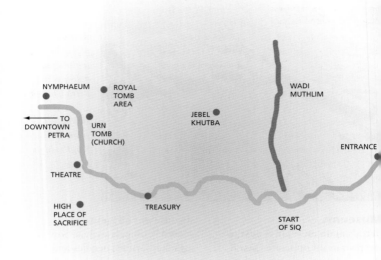

SITE MAP OF PETRA

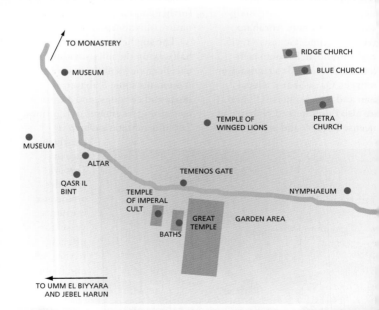

DOWNTOWN PETRA

TRAVEL INFORMATION

Petra is well prepared for the visitor and various forms of transport are available at every stage of the route, including horse drawn carriages. At the time of writing the horse ride down to the Siq is included in the price of the entry ticket. There are toilet facilities at strategic intervals, as well as places for refreshments, mostly reasonably priced. At the very end of the main section, next to the museum, there is a restaurant.

The official website for Petra is www. petrapark.com

See also www. nabataea.net which covers so much more than just Petra and the Nabataeans.

Hotels at all levels are adequate even at peak times. Although the main village, Wadi Musa, is a couple of kilometres away, there are always taxis at the entrance to the archaeological park. There are also hotels in the medium price range within walking distance of the entrance. The visitor can see a number of highlights in a day, but better to spend a night here. The round trip is roughly six hours from Amman and three hours from Aqaba.

To reach Petra from Amman drive on the airport highway until you reach the Petra turn-off about two hours from the airport. Petra is approximately three hours driving from Amman. It is also possible to go via the King's Highway, but this makes for a very long journey and if you do any site visiting on the way it can easily double the time it takes to get there.

It is important to make the **best use of the time** in Petra and plan in advance. Architecturally the similarity between the Khazneh and the Treasury could make the latter superfluous if you are limited for time. Better to visit the High Place of Sacrifice and the temples, particularly the Great Temple and Qasr el-Bint. The main 'cathedral' church is worth a visit and the other two are very nearby. The museum next to

the restaurant is perhaps the best place in Jordan for seeing Edomite and Nabataean artefacts and is well worth a twenty minute visit.

For the visitor with more than a day, one alternative route into the site is through Wadi Muthlim. Turn right just before the path enters the Siq, proceed along Wadi Muthlim until you eventually come to a T-junction where you take a left turn and head towards the end of this particular siq which will bring you out into an open area behind the royal tombs. This route should not be attempted in wet weather. Umm el-Biyyara rewards the visitor with great views, as does Jebel Haron which is a considerably longer round trip and takes a day.

8 The Valley—low living Canaanites

The lowest valley on earth has been a magnet for human settlement since earliest times because of its mild winter climate, water and lush vegetation

Baptism site and Elijah's hill

For the Christian, no visit to Jordan would be complete without a visit to the baptism site. The early church believed that this site was the 'Bethany on the other side of the Jordan' and was where Jesus was baptised (John 1:28). Many believe that it was in this general area that John was baptising, although we do not know exactly where Salim and Aenon were (John 3:23).

Partly because this area was in a security zone for many decades, it maintains something of its pristine wildness, although a number of denominations have built, or are building, churches at the site. Nearest the river is the gold-domed Orthodox church. The entrance fee includes the services of a mandatory guide and the use of an open top truck to get to the site. Visitors should be aware that if they have a Jordanian guide and transport with them they can see much more than on the standard tour. Elijah's hill (which can be pointed out from the truck) is well worth seeing and there are some interesting monk's dwellings carved out of the low hills just above the site, as well as other structures and pools associated with early pilgrims and solitaries who were attracted to the area.

It is possible to gain permission to be baptised in the river today, but this must be obtained in advance. The river itself is an international boundary between Jordan and Israel and therefore visitors at the river itself are always in the company of an unobtrusive but watchful soldier. Opposite is the Israeli site of Jesus' baptism and there are often

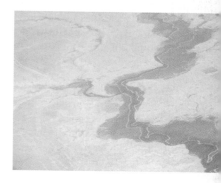

Above: *An aerial view of the river Jordan in which Jesus was baptised*

Facing page: *The Canaanite Gate shrine at Tell Zira'a*

fellow pilgrims on the other side separated by a few feet of water.

Situated on the edge of Wadi Kharrar, Elijah's hill is the traditional site for his transference to heaven (2 Kings 2: 4–12), which definitely took place on the east side of the river. On the hill and its immediate environs, part of the significant monastic presence in the area are three baptism pools, a prayer hall, cisterns, a Roman well and three churches. Of interest is the church built round a cave on the east side of the hill. Another church, with the mosaic inscription, is dedicated to 'Christ our God'. The well would have been there in the time of Christ even though the three pools and the churches date to the Byzantine period.

Going to the river area itself, the remains of three further Byzantine churches can be seen, with the third church—the one that we can see most of today—being built over the second. Because the river floods from time to time buildings were occasionally washed away. The unique design feature of the third church is an opening in the semi-circular apse leading down marble steps to what would in

Above: A visit to the baptism site also illustrates Jeremiah's words about the jungle or thicket of the Jordan (Jeremiah 12:5)

Below: The well on Elijah's hill. Coinage found on the site would date it to the time of Christ

those days have been the river itself (or its tributary). Also next to the old course of the river is the robing room where people waiting to be baptised would have changed before baptism. A short walk from these churches is the river itself and wooden steps lead down to a platform just above the surface, making it possible to dip one's feet in, or even gather, some Jordan river water!

Tell el-Hammam

Tell el-Hammam is a huge site, the largest Bronze Age city in the south Jordan Valley and is a serious candidate not just for biblical Sodom (see Box: Sodom and Gomorrah on page 108) but also Abel-Shittim.

The site was occupied before and during the time of Abraham, and was followed by a non-occupation gap of 500 years until the Iron Age. Steven Collins, who has devoted several seasons to the site, believes that in the Bronze Age it would have been a major fortified city-state with nearby towns and villages as its satellites, and that all these factors would be commensurate with it having been Sodom. During the early Bronze Age its walls were as much as 15m thick (50ft). It consists of an upper and lower tell and covers an area of 36 hectares (13 acres) including an area to the north and west of the site, by the stream. During the Iron Age only the upper tell was occupied. Even without entering the tell itself, significant Bronze Age ramparts made of mud brick, up to 10m high (33ft) and with an angle of 38 degrees, can be made out as well as wall lines.

As well as its possible identification with Sodom, it may well have been Abel-Shittim where a number of significant events took place; the Moabites corrupted the people of God (Numbers 25:1), the census of the Israelites took place (Numbers 26:3), Moses announced Joshua as his successor (Numbers 27:12–23), the eastern tribes received their allotment (Numbers 32), Moses delivered his final address (Deuteronomy 31:1) and Joshua sent out the spies (Joshua 2:1).

Opposite Tell el-Hammam, alongside the dam, are two late Hellenistic to early Roman fortresses. The first (Tell Barakat) is almost flush with, although at a higher elevation than, the actual dam wall, and the second excavated fort (Rujm Umm

Top right: The area of the three churches at the baptism site; notice the robing room in the foreground

Right: Part of the massive site of Tell el-Hammam; the upper tell is mainly Iron Age but the site extends all around it with very thick early Bronze Age walls

Left: View from Tell el-Hammam showing how fertile this area can be when there is water

Haddar) is a few hundred yards further on, atop a small hill, to the right of the road that goes round the dam. Rujm Umm Haddar has an interior cistern with original plastering and projecting corner towers.

Tell Nimrin

Although with little to see today, Tell Nimrin is probably Beth Nimrah, part of the inheritance of the tribe of Gad (Joshua 13:27). It seems to have been occupied first around the time of Abraham and could also have been biblical Admah (Genesis 14:2) if Sodom was located in the north. At that time a huge mud brick wall was built on top of stone foundations. After a 500 year gap in occupation, it was re-occupied

Sodom and Gomorrah

After separating from Abraham, Lot moved east settling in Sodom (Genesis 13:11–12). The debate over the exact location of Sodom has been re-ignited by excavations at Tell el-Hammam. The main theories put Sodom either at Bab edh-Dhra (see page 63), or at Tell el Hammam (see above), just north of the Dead Sea. The British Museum suggests Bab edh-Dhra as a possible location on the grounds that it reached its height of prosperity in the early Bronze Age and was finally abandoned around 2100 BC and never rebuilt. The location of the monastery complex of Deir Ain Abata (see pages 65-66) reflects a similar belief on the part of the early church. The first problem with this view is that the phrase the Kirkar, 'valley of the Jordan' (see Genesis 13:10,11) is always used of the circular area of the Jordan valley in the north and not in the south Dead Sea area. A second problem is that while there are indeed five identifiable ancient cities in the south (see Genesis 14:1–3) they had ceased to be significant by the time of the normally accepted dating for Abraham (around 2,000 BC at the earliest). Tell el-Hamman has a suitable archaeological profile and the size of the site would be commensurate with the importance of Sodom in the biblical narrative. There is also a 'gap' in occupation, whose beginning is consistent with the normally accepted dating for Abraham and also with a possible catastrophic event leading to instant depopulation.

The Balaam Inscription

Discovered in a religious sanctuary at Tell Dayr Alla in 1967 and written in coloured inks on plaster, the 7th or 8th century BC Aramaic inscription is a supposed prophecy of Balaam. It speaks of a council of displeased gods and of the doom awaiting the earth because of disorders in nature. The worldview is a polytheistic one but the 'gods' are not particularly concerned about evil. There are numerous parallels with, and contrasts to, the language and thought in the Old Testament. Two Old Testament names for God, 'El' and 'Shaddai' are used in the inscription. The language of judgement is similar to that of the Old Testament, such as Isaiah 13:10–11. Another two lines recall some of the teaching of Ecclesiastes about death. Some descriptions of 'the prophet Balaam' mirror those in the Numbers account. There seems to have been a 'cult' in the area associated with this false prophet who is mentioned around sixty times in Scripture, including three in the New Testament (2 Peter 2:15; Jude 11; Revelation 2:14). His crime in opposing Yahweh marked him out for destruction at the time of the conquest (Joshua 13:22). The actual inscription can be seen in the Amman museum.

Left: Part of the Balaam inscription.
© DoA. Jordan

in the Iron Age. It is situated at a cross-roads between an important east-west route through Wadi Shueib and the north-south valley route as well as being in the midst of a good agricultural land. At least one Byzantine church stood on the site and a hoard of Byzantine coins from the 4th to 6th centuries was found there. Also of interest is the presence of Ywh and yh (derivatives of Yahweh) in the names found on pottery shards discovered at the site

Dayr Alla

Tell Dayr Alla is a good candidate for the site of biblical Succoth (Genesis 33:17) but it has also proved an important site that has helped us understand the culture of the Old Testament better. It was on a major trading route between Egypt and the north,

Above: Part of the restored structures at Dayr Alla

and contained a shrine where the Balaam inscription was found and where people presented offerings for safe journeys during their trading activities. Later, the site was a centre of textile production and copper smelting with three smelting furnaces, built on top of each other, being discovered on the summit of the tell. It was between here (if this was Succoth) and Tell Saidiyeh (if that was Zarethan) that King Solomon centred his copper smelting activities; the presence of furnaces on the tell confirms its suitability for such work (1 Kings 7:45–46).

Today, there has been modern restoration using modern mud bricks and it is therefore possible to obtain an idea of what some structures on the site would have looked like. As well as its famous inscription, the site has yielded a rich harvest of written material including, unusually, two pieces in an unknown language.

The international nature of the pottery discovered here points to Dayr Alla's important position on trading routes over a long period of time. There is a small museum at the site in the former excavation house which can be visited if the curator is available.

Tulul adh-Dhahab and the Jabbok river

On either side of the Jabbok river, after an attractive 9km (5 ½ mi) drive east of Tell Dayr Alla, are the twin hills of Tulul adh-Dhahab ,both of which are substantial sites. Early on in the journey by the river, soon after the military checkpoint, is one of the world's oldest iron smelting sites, Tell Hammeh, whose smelting activities date back to the 10th century BC and from which it is still possible to pick up the odd piece of iron slag. According to the experts, it has all the features

necessary for iron smelting: water, clay, wind and iron ore (from a nearby mine). It stands on a little rise behind dilapidated buildings.

Reaching the twin tells of Tulul adh-Dhahab, Tell adh-Dhahab al-Garbiyya (the west tell) has traditionally been taken as the site of Peniel, where Jacob wrestled with God (Genesis 32:30). If this was Peniel, it was also the site of Jeroboam's eastern capital (1 Kings 12:25). Recent excavations have opened up the possibility that adh-Dhahab al-Garbiyya could also be the site of the Herodian fortress of Amathus. The remains of a Hellenistic colonnaded courtyard (temenos) on the summit and defensive walls, including a fine glacis (a steeply sloping section of fortification) halfway up the hill, could point to a Herodian castle similar to Machaerus (see pages 52-53). On the south west of the summit, a little lower down, a tower has been uncovered dated to between 1300 and 1000 BC. Re-used Iron Age carvings of a woman and a lion (or child with goat!) point to the presence of a religious shrine on the summit from the 8th or 9th centuries BC. On the opposite hill of Tell adh-Dhahab ash-Sharqiyya (the east tell) parts of a square building are clearly visible probably dating to the Iron Age. There are also wall lines including an extensive one leading up from the river.

Tell adh-Dhahab ash-Sharqiyya (the east tell) has been identified with biblical Mahanaim where David fled to (2 Samuel 17:24); but has not been excavated. The two hills of

Tulul adh-Dhahab are well worth visiting for the beauty of their surroundings and the importance of the sites. Although their identity is a matter of probability rather than certainty, that of the river Jabbok (Genesis 32:22) is beyond doubt.

Top: *Part of the glacis wall at adh-Dhahab al-Garbiyya*

Above: *Stairway to the spring at Saidiyeh*

Opposite page: *Jabbok valley and river. It was in this region that Jacob wrestled with God*

Above: The contents of a Tell Saidiyeh scullery c.2750 BC

Tell Saidiyeh

In spite of the erosion of the excavated areas, Tell Saidiyeh is worth visiting for its location at one of the narrowest points of the Jordan Valley and its proposed identification with biblical Zarethan, where the waters were stopped so that the people of Israel were able to cross the river opposite Jericho (Joshua 3:16). It lies in fertile land, at a cross-road of two major trade routes. A palace complex, dating to nearly a thousand years before Abraham, was discovered on the lower tell where olive oil, wine and textile production took place. From the late Bronze Age, Egyptian administrative buildings were found on the upper tell. There is an impressive restored stairway that led down to a well, where water continues to flow thousands of years after the original protective wall was built around it. On the lower western part of the tell there was also a graveyard.

During one of the last seasons of excavation at the site, a kitchen was discovered with table settings for eleven people; the impression was of a meal that had been hastily abandoned. The contents of the kitchen (or scullery) dated to 2750 BC can be seen today at the British Museum. With the now carbonised foods they ate, this is an excellent insight into everyday life of the Canaanites in the early Bronze Age.

Right: The wadi Yabis which is a possible candidate for the brook Cherith

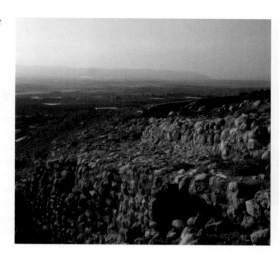

Right: Wall lines at Tell Abu Kharaz. Possibly Jabesh Gilead. However, the men who brought back the corpses of Saul and Jonathan would not have taken a whole night to get from Beisan (Beth Shan), clearly visible on the other side of the valley, to Tell Abu Kharaz (1 Samuel 31:12)

Tell Abu Kharaz

Tell Abu Kharaz (possibly Jabesh Gilead) is a significant and steeply-sided site with wide ranging views over the valley to the north and south. You can see the hills around Nazareth, Mount Tabor, the Samarian hills, Beth Shan, and the beginning of the valley of Jezreel. The summit area is around 1.5 hectares (3.7 acres) and it is one of the largest sites in the central Jordan Valley. It is situated almost 250m below sea level. The soil around it is fertile and it is near the perennial stream known today as Wadi Yabis (which may be the brook Cherith of 1 Kings 17:3) and the river Jordan. The population was at its highest before Abraham and the site was then unoccupied for 1,200 years, but later was reoccupied during the Middle Bronze age.

Tell Abu Kharaz was a wealthy city as evidenced by the remains found there, and had extensive trading contacts with Egypt, Lebanon and beyond. A Middle to Late Bronze bakery was discovered, and among the material finds from the tell was a god figure

Left: The Canaanite temple at Pella

Above: A view of the civic centre church, Odeum and baths from the citadel at Pella.

with the legs of a lion reminiscent of the figure in Daniel 2:31–49. Today there is a well restored section of the massive Early Bronze defensive wall, topped by a Middle to Late Bronze section in the southern part of the summit. This was completed by mud brick and wood, and reached an estimated height of 6 to 8 metres; there is a tunnel opening between the walls. In the south west of the tell a temple was discovered with steps leading up to it. A square, free-standing altar was found here. Other structures from the Bronze and Iron ages are visible at the site which is particularly worth visiting in spring for the hills are crowned with green.

Pella

The Pella area has a record of semi-continuous habitation from the Stone Age until the present day. It is in a dream location at the centre of three eco-systems: hills, temperate sea level land and a sub-tropical valley with good winter rainfall in the hills and a perennial stream. Strategically, it was at the cross-road of important

Top left: A small iron age altar from Pella with two representations of Astarte acting as columns at the bottom of the picture

Left: A view of Tell Zira'a in the spring

north-south and east-west routes.
The two main parts are the citadel
hill and the main site below. Pella
was an important Bronze and
Iron Age site, evidenced by its
mention in around 100 ancient
texts. It was also a Decapolis city
from the time of Christ, but one
whose visible Roman remains
are a little sparse today. Josephus
and Eusebius record that the
early Christians, in obedience to
Matthew 24:16, fled to Pella just
before the fall of Jerusalem in AD
70. Its large fortress temple and
its beautiful location are good
reasons for a visit. On a clear day
it is possible to see Mount Gilboa
where Saul and his sons died in
battle, 1 Samuel 31), the entrance
to the valley of Jezreel (1 Kings
21:1), Mount Tabor (Psalm 89:12)
and the outskirts of Nazareth,
the hill where Nain (Luke 7:11)
was situated, as well as a whole
swathe of the Jordan Valley.

A visit can begin with the main
civic complex which contains a
significant church. Nearby, is
the semi-circular small theatre,
or Odeum, which must have had
its counterpart elsewhere on the
site, in a full scale

theatre; however this is so far
undiscovered. Climbing the hill
and walking towards the west,
the visitor passes the main site
on the right which in Abraham's
day would have been surrounded
by an impressive mud brick wall
and would have enclosed eight
hectares of land and a probable
population of 2,000.

Eventually, the fortress temple
is reached higher on the hill. It
was similar in design to, but larger
than, the one found at Shechem
(Judges 9:46–49) and its basic
dimensions were 32 by 24m (104
by 78ft). This fortress temple
could have been 10m (33ft) high,
of three or four storeys, with mud
brick and timber used for the
upper storeys. Two large towers
flanked the eastern entrance. The
temple was originally built in
1600 BC, partially destroyed in an
earthquake in 1350 BC, rebuilt in
950 BC and then destroyed around
800 BC. Its religious nature has
been confirmed by its design and
the cultic objects found inside.

The views from the citadel
are more spectacular than those
from the main site and the best

*Right: It is thought
that beside the gate
in the casemate wall
at Tell Zira'a was a
gate shrine marked
by two basalt
pillar bases and a
(probable) sacred
stone which can be
seen to the right of
the basalt stones*

way of approach is to drive round the back of the citadel where there are some interesting Romano-Byzantine tombs that can be entered, and a couple of milestones to be seen. There were significant Byzantine buildings on the citadel but also material from earlier periods.

Tell Zira'a

Tell Zira'a is a strategically situated site with occupation over a period of around 5,000 years. It overlooked an important route linking the Jordan Valley with the highlands of Bashan. The Wadi Arab dam immediately in front of the tell, adds to the attractiveness of the location. It also had its own water supply in the form of an internal well, which can still be seen today. Some of the most impressive remains of Tell Zira'a include a fine casemate wall dating from the Late Bronze Age. At that time it could well have been the centre of a city-state. The houses within the wall may have been two storeys. Situated in the Jordan Valley area, the discoveries of religious objects are consistent with it being a Canaanite city. Among the figures found at the site were a Bronze Age 'Astarte', an Iron Age 'El' and a seal of Baal sitting on a bull. After less organised occupation in the earlier part of the Iron Age, there was subsequent occupation as a walled city during the later Iron Age. In the north of the tell five Romano-Byzantine houses and a paved street have been excavated.

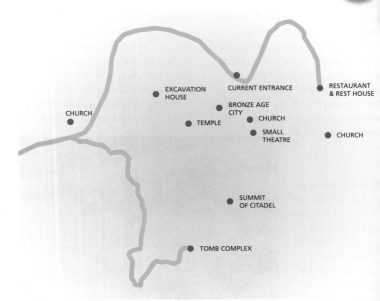

CHURCH

EXCAVATION HOUSE

CURRENT ENTRANCE

RESTAURANT & REST HOUSE

BRONZE AGE CITY

TEMPLE

CHURCH

SMALL THEATRE

CHURCH

SUMMIT OF CITADEL

TOMB COMPLEX

SITE MAP OF PELLA

For **the baptism site**, take the airport highway and turn off for the Dead Sea. At the former checkpoint, which is at the sign for sea level, make sure you take the **left turn** signposted for the Dead Sea. The way to the baptism site is reasonably well signposted. The first tour at the site sets off at 8.30 am and the last at 3.00pm in winter and 5.00pm in summer (April to October inclusive).

Website: www.baptismsite.com
☎ 0777607032.

For Tell el-Hammam take the right turn at the Dead Sea checkpoint on the main road to the Dead Sea from Amman. It is next to the 'Sea Level' sign. You will come to the dam on your right after a couple of kilometres and Tell el-Hammam is on your left. Website: www.tallelhammam.com. Prior permission is needed to visit this site.
☎ 053570412
mobile ☎ 0777723056).

Tell Nimrin is almost opposite the police station as you enter South Shuna along the Wadi Shueib road that descends from the town of Salt. The road cuts into the tell, disclosing some of the walls but there is little to see otherwise.

Deir Alla, Tulul adh-Dhahab, Tell Saidiyeh, Abu Kharaz and **Pella** are all off the main Jordan Valley road. The conspicuous tell of Dayr Alla is behind a petrol station as you come north out of the town of Dayr Alla. Opposite Tell Dayr Alla is a road that goes east weaving along the river for about 9km (5½mi) and will take you to **Tulul ad-Dhahab** The turn off for **Tell Saidiyeh** is unmarked but is 8.5km north of Tell Dayr Alla. Turn left opposite a mosque. You can see the long tell from the main road. **Tell Abu Kharaz** is 24.5km north of Tell Dayr Alla along the main road and you turn to the right opposite the Wadi Rayan municipality building. The tell is on the nearest hill. The marked turn-off for

Above: Another view the Jordan river; it easy to understand Naaman's rather contemptuous remarks about this insignificant river (1 Kings 5:12)

Pella is a little further on to your right after you go through the village of Masharia.

Tell Zira'a is most easily reached from Umm Queis. Take the road going south from Umm Queis, opposite the car park for the site of Umm Queis, and follow it for a few kilometres and you will eventually come to the site on your right. It has a flattish top and is unmistakable.

The timeline of Archaeological periods

Neolithic (Stone Age) to 4500

Chalcolithic (copper and stone) 4500–3300

Early Bronze Age	3300–2400	
Early Bronze Age IV	2400–2000	
Middle Bronze Age	2000–1550	Abraham, Isaac, Jacob
Late Bronze Age	1550–1200	Moses, Joshua, Judges
Iron Age 1	1200–1000	Saul and David
Iron Age 2	1000–586	The divided monarchy and the prophets
Babylonian	586–539	The later Judean monarchy and fall of Jerusalem
Persian	539–332	The return from exile. Esther, Ezra, Nehemiah
Hellenistic (Greek)	332–141	Between the Testaments
Roman	37 BC–AD 324	The life of Jesus Christ and the early Christian church
Byzantine	324–640	Christian period
Islamic expansion	632	Leading to the Ottoman Empire 1299–1922

Peoples of the land

Peoples	Page number	Peoples	Page number
Arabs	28	Edomites	78
Ammonites	37	Moabites	65
Amorites	21	Nabataeans	93
Canaanites	22		

Above: *South Theatre at Jerash*

FURTHER READING

Blue Guide to Jordan (3rd edition). Rollins and Streetly. A & C Black. Dated but with a mass of valuable architectural and archaeological information. Obtainable second hand via the internet.

East of the Jordan. Burton Macdonald. American Schools of Oriental Research. Invaluable for site identification. The book can be downloaded free from the internet. Burton has also written **Pilgrimage in Early Christian Jordan** (Bannerstone Press)

Rough Guide to Jordan (4th edition). Matthew Teller. Rough Guides (Penguin). For backpackers but also good site information on major places and good city maps.

Petra. Jane Taylor. Aurum Press. Also published in Jordan by Al-Uzza press. Good introduction to Petra and the Nabataeans.

AUTHOR

Edward Dawson studied at All Nations Christian College and has an MTh in Church History from Kings College, London. He has taught for some years at Jordan Evangelical Theological Seminary, including a course on the Biblical Geography of Jordan and Syria. He has been visiting sites in Jordan associated with the Bible for over twenty years, and is currently resident in Jordan.

ACKNOWLEDGEMENTS

Mark Connally has had a large influence on the book as well as contributing some of the pictures from his Middle East photo-archive.

The Director and staff at the American Centre for Oriental Research in Amman, in whose library the book was researched and written.

Brian Edwards for his courteous and efficient editing.

Jordanian Friends of Archaeology and Heritage with whom I first visited some of these sites.

Picture acknowledgements

Although the author's own, the ten pictures from Jordan museums are included here by kind permission of the Jordanian Department of Antiquities.

The 'Roman army' pictures on pages 21-22 are by kind permission of the Roman Army and Chariot experience, Jerash, Jordan

Right: Coloured sand from Petra

Above: *The Great Temple at Petra*

TRAVEL INFORMATION FOR JORDAN

The official Jordan tourism site www.visitjordan.com

www.jordanjubilee.com is also an excellent source of general information.

Archaeological sites

Some of the sites in this book are definitely not on the normal tourist route, but information on them is given because of their interest to Bible students and also on the understanding that visitors will respect the sites which sometimes represent work in progress. This means not walking on the actual ruins themselves and staying outside the excavated squares. Sometimes a caretaker will come up and accompany you on your visit.

Visa and currency

Anyone from a Western country will be able to obtain a visa on arrival to be purchased in dinars. The Jordanian dinar is pegged to the US dollar and is roughly the same as a pound sterling.

When changing money try and get some smaller denomination notes as change is sometimes a problem. ATMS are widely available in Amman and other major cities. Major credit cards are accepted at more tourist oriented places. Travellers cheques can be difficult to cash.

Climate

Spring (March and April) is the loveliest time to visit Jordan with its intense, and relatively brief, flowering period. Autumn is also pleasant but can be dry and dusty. From November to April there may be warm days but around 25 weather fronts hit the country and the visitor needs to be prepared for rainy weather even during the spring season. Snow is possible, particularly in January or February, but in most areas it does not settle. The Jordan Valley and Aqaba are sub-tropical. You will have temperatures in the 40°C in the Jordan Valley in summer. Amman and the highlands will typically be in the low thirties in summer but hot spells are possible when it can be as much as 40°C for a week or so.

Dress

It is wise to dress modestly and avoid tight fitting or revealing clothing. Except perhaps for Aqaba, it is best even for men not to wear shorts and they are not acceptable for women. Normal swimwear is fine for Aqaba and the Dead Sea. Visitors should not take their cues from the behaviour and dress of some Jordanians in West Amman which is an island in an otherwise conservative country. During the summer you should wear some headgear. The local Arab headdress, the kefiyeh (called a 'hatta' in Jordan) can help keep you cool especially when periodically dipped in water. During the winter months rainwear and warm clothing are needed.

Car Hire

Car Hire is straightforward with a Western driving licence. Extra care is needed in driving because the rate of traffic accidents is relatively high in the Middle East. Driving is on the right.

Taxis and buses and serveeses

In Amman, make sure the driver turns on the meter which at the time of writing starts at 250, a quarter of a dinar (the dinar was originally divided into 1,000 fils). In Amman even the longest journey is unlikely to be more than 3 dinars. For a taxi to take you outside Amman you will need to negotiate and fix details of the journey a day in advance as the driver needs a permit for this. 'Serveeses' are white, shared, fixed route, fixed price taxis. You pay the same wherever you join them. Grey 'mumaayaz' taxis are more expensive than the yellow ones. There is a good bus system both within and outside Amman, but for many sites buses are not practical unless you have unlimited time and are prepared to do a lot of walking.

Security

Jordan is a very safe and welcoming country for tourists and the King and Government intend to keep it so. There are tourist police at the main sites.

Above: *Street scene in Salt*

Above: The Nabataean experience—Nabataean food from Petra

Photography

Be careful not to take photographs near military or police checkpoints, airports and in other sensitive security areas. Like most people, locals going about their business do not like being seen as animals in a zoo and it is wise always to ask permission before photographing people. As a man, you should never ask a Muslim woman for permission to photograph her, but sometimes it works when a woman does.

Carrying passports

For the Jordan Valley, the Dead Sea, the northern Umm Queis area and Aqaba you must carry your passport. A driving licence with your photo is normally sufficient in the unlikely event you are asked for identification in other areas.

Food and Drink

Drinking bottled water is best if you are on a short visit. More and more local people use it. It is wise to avoid uncooked vegetables, even in hotels, and to avoid buying unbranded food and drink from street vendors.

Medical and hygiene

Jordan is a regional health centre and the standard of medical care is good. Insurance is recommended. Typhoid and Hepatitis A inoculations are advisable before coming to Jordan.

Anti-bacterial hand-wash solutions are widely available and should be regularly used.

Tipping and bargaining

Where there is no service charge, tipping at meals is expected at around 10%. On tours the going rate seems to be US$3 a day per person for the guide and US$2 a day for the driver. A growing number of tourist shops have fixed prices displayed. Where there are no prices displayed, get advice from your guide or someone in the hotel about going rates for items. Or ask the 'price' at more than one shop. Many readers of this book will be from the relatively wealthy west and should keep a sense of proportion when they bargain, remembering that it is the Jordanian vendor's livelihood. In most cases a transaction can be carried out that is reasonably fair to both parties especially if you can talk to a local beforehand.

Electricity and internet

Continental 2 pin sockets are used. Internet access is not an issue as more and more hotels offer Wi-fi and there are internet cafes everywhere.

Right: *The ceremonial way, and modern steps, up Jabel Khutba at Petra*

Below: *Residential Amman*

DAY ONE TRAVEL GUIDES

This series is unique: each book combines biography an history with travel guide. Notes, maps and photographs help you to explore Britain's distinctive heritage.

ALSO AVAILABLE

Through the British Mueum: with the Bible

Discover the many Bible related exhibits at Britain's most popular tourist destination.

128 pages

- PLACES OF INTEREST
- PACKED WITH COLOUR PHOTOS
- CLEAR ILLUSTRATED MAPS
- GREAT GIFT IDEA

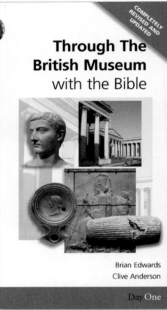

COMPLETELY REVISED AND UPDATED

Through The British Museum
with the Bible

Brian Edwards
Clive Anderson

Day One

ORDER TODAY

CALL DAYONE PUBLICATIONS ON ☎ 01568 613740 AND ORDER TODAY

A series of children's activity books twinned with the Travel Guides

ROMANS, GLADIATORS AND GAMES
In the British Museum, explore the Roman world of the first Christians.

KINGS, PHARAOHS AND BANDITS
In the British Museum, explore the world of Abraham to Esther.

WILLIAM TYNDALE
He was threatened, hunted, betrayed and killed so that we could have the Bible in English

Permission is given to copy the activity pages and associated text for use as class or group material

JOHN BUNYAN
How a hooligan and solidier became a preacher, prisoner and famous writer

WILLIAM CAREY
The story of a country boy and shoe mender whose big dreams took him to India

WILLIAM BOOTH
The troublesome teenager who changed the lives of people no one else would touch

WILLIAM WILBERFORCE
The millionaire child who worked so hard to win the freedom of African slaves.

C S LEWIS
The story of one of the world's most famous authors who sold over a hundred million books

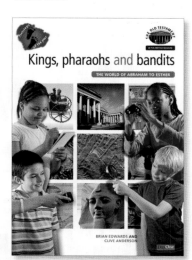

OTHER TITLES IN THIS SERIES

Travel with...

JOHN BUNYAN
C H SPURGEON
WILLIAM BOOTH
JOHN KNOX
MARTYN LLOYD-JONES
WILLIAM GRIMSHAW
WILLIAM CAREY
WILLIAM WILBERFORCE
C S LEWIS
ROBERT MURRAY McCHEYNE
MARTYRS OF MARY TUDOR
JOHN CALVIN
WILLIAM TYNDALE
JOHN BLANCHARD
BILLY GRAHAM
FRANCES RIDLEY HAVERGAL

Travel through...

THE BRITISH MUSEUM
OXFORD
CAMBRIDGE
ISRAEL
EGYPT

MORE TITLES ARE IN PREPARATION

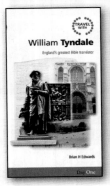

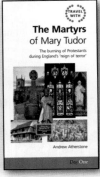

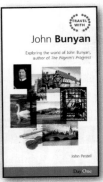